ENGLISHSKILLS

ONE

WITH AN AUDIO-CD

Dr. Muhammad Ali Alkhuli

Publisher: DAR ALFALAH	الناشر: دار الفلاح للنشر والتوزيع
P. O. Box 818	ص. ب 818
Swaileh 11910	صويلح 11910
Jordan	الأردن
Tel & Fax 009626-5411547	هاتف وفاكس 009626-5411547

E-mail: books@daralfalah.com

Website: www.daralfalah.com

Copyright: by the Publisher

All rights are reserved.

2005 Edition

Publisher: DAR ALFALAH	الناشر: دار الفلاح للنشر والتوزيع
P. O. Box 818	ص. ب 818
Swaileh 11910	صويلح 11910
Jordan	الأردن
Tel & Fax 009626-5411547	هاتف وفاكس 009626-5411547

E-mail: books@daralfalah.com
Website: www.daralfalah.com

رقم الإيداع لدى دائرة المكتبة الوطنية
2003/6/1055

420.71
KHU Alkhuli, Muhammad Ali
English Skills One, Muhammad Ali Alkhuli.
Amman: Dar Al-Falah for Publishing and Distributing,
    2003.
172 pages
Deposit No. 2003/5/1055
Descriptors:/English Language//Second Language
    Learning/

** تم إعداد بيانات الفهرسة والتصنيف الأولية من قبل دائرة المكتبة الوطنية، عمّان، الأردن

رقم الإجازة المتسلسل لدى دائرة المطبوعات والنشر 2003/6/1070

| ISBN | 9 9 5 7 – 4 0 1 – 5 0 – 5 | (ردمك) |

بسم الله الرحمن الرحيم

CONTENTS

PREFACE

This book is intended to be used for a university freshman course usually called "English 1", given to students as an obligatory university requirement. The book contains fourteen units, one for each week of the semester if possible. However, the instructor may select whatever units that suit his students' level and the time available. To add, this book can be used for reading and comprehension courses.

Each unit contains one passage divided into three parts: two for reading comprehension and one for listening comprehension. The passage is followed by exercises on eight language skills or sub-skills: reading, listening, vocabulary, grammar, punctuation, spelling, pronunciation, and free writing.

Each unit has sixteen exercises: Exercise 1 and Exercise 2 on reading comprehension, Exercise 3 on listening comprehension, Exercises 4-6 on vocabulary, Exercises 7-9 on grammar, Exercise 10 on punctuation, Exercises 11-13 on spelling, Exercises 14-15 on pronunciation, and finally Exercise 16 on free writing.

This book is designed with these considerations in mind:

1. The reading material level is selected to suit university students in the Arab Word, i.e., a level a little higher than the secondary-stage level.

2. The topics of the passages are made as varied as possible so as to suit the different majors of freshman students at universities such as science, arts, and business.

3. The reading passage is divided into three parts so as to make comprehension easier . The focus will be on only one

paragraph or two in each part at a time, instead of all the passage as one piece.

4. The language activities, skills, and exercises are meant to be comprehensive: reading comprehension, listening comprehension, vocabulary, grammar, punctuation, spelling, pronunciation, and free writing. Thus, most language skills and sub-skills are taken care of.

5. The fourteen passages are arranged according to their level of difficulty, starting with the easy and ending with the less easy.

6. Answers are to be written on the spaces provided in every exercises.

7. An audio-CD recorded by a native speaker is available, which makes this book usable for courses on listening comprehension as well.

Author

Dr. Muhammad Ali Alkhuli

How to Use the Book

To use this book efficiently, it is better to follow these recommendations:

1. Students are to read each part in the passage silently and separately, and then they answer the comprehension questions on that part. In other words, they read Part 1 and then they do exercise 1 immediately. Then they go to Part 2 and do Exercise 2.

2. As for Part 3, students are to close their books and listen to their instructor while reading this part. Then they do Exercise 3. This part is meant to be a listening practice. However, if this activity does not suit the students for some reason, Part 3 may be used for reading comprehension instead of listening comprehension. Each of the previous exercises, i.e., Exercises 1-3, has 4-6 questions, but the instructor can, of course, add many more if he chooses to.

3. Vocabulary exercises (4-6) are text-tied and include different types of activities such as word matching, synonyms, antonyms, derivations, suffixes, and prefixes.

4. Grammar exercises (7-9) review 42 grammatical patterns all through the book, three patterns in each unit, and they are text-tied in most cases.

5. Punctuation exercises in the book review all punctuation marks, graded and accumulated all through. Exercise 10 in each unit is meant to deal with punctuation.

6. As for spelling, there are three exercises in each unit that deal with spelling .n Exercise 11 usually gives a spelling rule,

which requires some explanation before doing the exercise. Exercise 12 calls for spelling practice of selected words from the unit text; each word has to be written once or more for practice purposes. Exercise 13 is a dictation exercise based on a selection from the passage. Here the instructor selects a paragraph or a part of it and gives it as a dictation practice. He may select separate words if he chooses to do so.

7. As for pronunciation, Exercise 14 usually gives a pronunciation rule, which needs to be discussed first before doing the drill. As for Exercise 15, it is usually a stress drill, where the instructor may give the model first, and then students may repeat.

8. Finally, there is Exercise 16 on free writing. A paragraph is expected to be written freely, or a summary of the passage is required. Exercise 16 is text-tied, i.e., dependent on the passage. This exercise can be done at home and later discussed in class. There is nothing obligatory here; the instructor is to use his own discretion and experienced judgment. Whether this exercise is to be done or not depends on the time available, the students' level and motivation, and more importantly on the instructor's judgment.

9. In all the sixteen exercises of each unit, enough spaces are provided for writing the answers.

10. The instructor may cover all the fourteen units of this book or may select any number of them, depending on the students' interest and level, and on the time available.

11. Most of the sixteen exercises, if not all, are text-tied, i.e., text-dependent. They are tied to the passages of the units.

12. It is often the case that a very brief note, rule, or explanation is given before many exercises. These notes are not meant to be detailed or complete, nor can they be so here.

13. If a certain unit is found to be too difficult for a certain class, it may be skipped, and an easier unit may be selected instead.

The Author
Dr. Muhammad Ali Alkhuli

Unit 1

The MIGRATION OF BIRDS

(1)

Here is a scientific experiment on the homing of birds, the facts of which are quite certain. A few years ago seven swallows were caught near their nests at Bremen in Germany. They were marked with a red dye on some of their white feathers, so that they could easily be seen. Then they were taken by aeroplane to
5   Croydon, near London; this is a distance of 400 miles.

The seven swallows were set free at Croydon. Five of them flew back to their nests at Bremen. How did the birds find their way on that long journey, which they had never made before? That is the great puzzle. It is no good saying that the swallows

10   have a 'sense of direction', or an 'instinct to go home'. These are just words, and explain nothing. We want to know exactly what senses the animals use to find their way and how they know in which direction to go until they can see familiar **landmarks**. Unfortunately, practically no **scientific experiments** have yet been made on this question.

(2)

15   Perhaps migrating birds are the greatest mystery of all. Swallows leave England in August and September, and they fly to Africa, where they stay during our winter . The swallows return to England in the spring, to nest. There are other birds too that leave England in the late summer for the south. A lot has been found out about the journeys of **migrating birds** by marking the birds with aluminum rings put on one
20   leg. An address and a number are put on the ring.

Swallows from England go as far as South Africa; and as many as fourteen birds, marked with rings in England, have been

caught again in South Africa. From England to South Africa is a journey of 6,000

25   miles. And the birds not only return from Africa to England next spring, but

often they come back to nest in the very same house where they nested the year

before.

(3)

How do the birds find their way on these enormously long journeys? The

young birds are not taught the road by their parents because the parents often fly

30   off first. We have no idea how the birds find their way, particularly as many of

them fly by night, when **landmarks** could hardly be seen. And other birds

migrate over the sea, where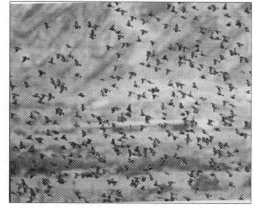

there are no landmarks at all. A

certain kind of plover, for

35   instance, nests in Canada. At

the end of the summer these

birds migrate from Canada to

South America; they fly 2,500

miles, non-stop, over the

40   ocean. Not only is this very

long flight an extraordinary

feat of endurance, but there

are no landmarks on the ocean to guide the birds.

It has been suggested that birds can sense the magnetic lines of force

45   stretching from the north to south **magnetic poles** of the earth, and so direct

themselves. But all experiments hitherto made to see whether magnetism has any

effect whatsoever on animals have given negative results. Still, where there is

such a **biological mystery** as migration, even improbable experiments are worth

trying. Research was being done in Poland on the possible influence of

50   **magnetism** on path-finding. Magnets were attached to the birds' heads to see

whether their direction-sense was confused thereby.

Reading Comprehension

Exercise 1 | Part 1

Read Part 1 silently, and then answer these questions.

1. How many birds were included in the experiment?

    _____

2. Where was the home of the swallows?

    _____

3. How were the birds taken to Croydon?

    _____

4. How many birds could not return to Germany?

    _____

5. What is the purpose of this experiment?

    _____

Exercise 2 | Part 2

Read Part 2 silently, and then answer these questions.

1. Why do birds migrate from England in August?

    _____

2. When do the swallows return to England?

    _____

3. How are the birds marked?

    _____

4. How many kilometers is the distance between England and South Africa?

    _____

5.   Do the birds return to the same house?

_____

Close your book, and listen to your instructor reading   Part 3. Then determine if these statements are true or false according to the text.

1.   Parents do not teach young birds how to fly back home.

_____

2.   Landmarks on the sea guide birds back home.

_____

3.   The distance from Canada to South America is 2.500 miles.

_____

4.   Birds can surely sense the magnetic lines of the earth.

_____

5.   How birds go back home is still a mystery.

_____

Vocabulary

Find for the words in List A their synonyms in List B.

List A   List B

1. set free   _____   **a.** effect

2. instance   _____   **b.** example

3. journey   _____   **c.** great deed

4. influence   _____   **d.** release

5. feat   _____   **e.** trip

                                              f. endurance

Exercise 5	Noun Derivation

Derive a noun from each of these words by adding a suitable suffix.

1. migrate   _____   5. fly   _____

2. mark   _____   6. attach   _____

3. return   _____   7. explain   _____

4. improbable _____   8. possible   _____

Exercise 6	Word Selection

Fill in the blanks with one of these words in its right form: magnetism, endurance, migrate, experiment, biology, magnetic, direct.

1. The plover is a _____ bird that flies to South America every summer.

2. Science mainly depends on _____.

3. This is a strong car with high _____.

4. Some believe that there is a _____ watch inside every human being.

5. There is a special kind of _____ in his eyes

Grammar

Exercise 7 | Form 2 and Form 3

There are two types of verbs: regular and irregular. **Regular verbs** take **-ed** for Form 2 and Form 3, e.g., learn, learn**ed**, learn**ed**. **Irregular verbs** do not take **-ed,** and they have some internal changes, e.g., write, wrote, written.

Give the past form and the past participle form of each verb.

1. make _____ _____   6. nest _____ _____

2. ring _____ _____   7. see _____ _____

3. come _____ _____   8. swim _____ _____

4. fly _____ _____   9. influence _____ _____

5. invade _____ _____   10. sense _____ _____

Exercise 8 | Some and Any

"**Some**" is usually used in affirmative statements ."**Any**" is usually used in questions and negative statements.

Add some **or** any **in each blank.**

1.   The bird lost _____ of its feathers.

2.   He doesn't have _____ idea about the subject

3.   _____ countries are cold, but _____ are hot.

4.   I don't see _____ nests on this tree.

5.   He needs _____ books, but he doesn't need _____ copybooks.

Exercise 9 | Statement → Question

> To change a statement into a **yes-no question**, front the auxiliary if there is one, or add **do, does, or did** if there is no auxiliary. In both cases, the **auxiliary** comes before the subject, e.g., He will come ⟹ Will he come?

Change these statements into yes-no questions.

1. They can mark the birds with a red dye.

   _____

2. The birds found their way back.

   _____

3. The swallow returns to England in Spring.

   _____

4. They have no idea how the birds find their way.

   _____

5. The results of the experiments were negative.

   _____

Punctuation

Exercise 10 | Capital Letters

> **Capital letters** are used at the sentence beginning, at a quotation beginning, and **initially** with the names of persons, countries, cities, rivers, seas, oceans, mountains, days, lakes, streets, ships, and titles.

Capitalize the letters that have to be capitalized.

1. the nile is the only river in egypt.

    _____

2. birds fly from england to south africa and from canada to south america.

    _____

3. he asked, "why is she late?"

    _____

4. the red sea is between the mediterranean sea and the indian ocean.

    _____

5. damascus is the capital of syria.

    _____

ABCDEFGHI JKLMN	**Spelling and Dictation**	OPQRSTUV WXYZ

Exercise 11	**The Final y**

> If a word ends in *-y* preceded by a consonant and a suffix beginning with a vowel is added, *y* becomes *i,* e.g., *lady + es → ladies.* If *y* is preceded by a vowel, *y* remains *y,* e.g., *journeys.*

Combine these units changing y into i wherever necessary.

1. country + es = _____   6. academy + es = _____

2. storey + s = _____   7. hurry + ed = _____

3. carry + ed = _____   8. carry + er = _____

4. navy + es = _____   9. journey + s = _____

5. toy + s = _____   10. way + s = _____

Exercise 12	Practice

Practice the spelling of these words.

1. experiment   _____   6. magnetism   _____

2. feather   _____   7. practically   _____

3. aluminum   _____   8. journey   _____

4. enormously   _____   9. themselves   _____

5. extraordinary   _____   10. address   _____

Exercise 13	Dictation

You may have any paragraph in the passage or a part of it as a dictation exercise, depending on your instructor's choice.

Pronunciation

Exercise 14	The Final e

*The **final silent e** makes the **medial vowel in monosyllabic words** be pronounced the way it is named, e.g., fine, hate.*

Pronounce these words, and re-write them.

1. sit, site   _____   6. can, cane   _____

2. bit, bite	_____	7. car, care	_____
3. wit, white	_____	8. kit, kite	_____
4. rat, rate	_____	9. fin, fine	_____
5. fat, fate	_____	10. mat, mate	_____

Exercise 15	Stress

Pronounce and re-write these words, putting the strong stress on the right syllable, e.g., meáning.

1. scientific	_____	6. Africa	_____
2. confused	_____	7. animal	_____
3. improbable	_____	8. research	_____
4. instinct	_____	9. summer	_____
5. swallows	_____	10. distance	_____

Free Writing

Exercise 16	Paragraph Writing

Write a paragraph of about ten lines on the migration of birds. The topic sentence may run like this: There are several theories that try to explain how birds migrate and return home safely.

_____

_____

_____

_____

_____

_____

_____

_____

_____

_____

Unit 2

THE USE OF THE
COMPASS

(1)

We have seen how it is possible to find direction by means of landmarks, the sun, and the stars. But it may easily happen on a foggy day or a cloudy night that none of these can be seen. How does the traveler on land or the sailor on the sea find his way then? He uses an instrument called a **compass**.

5   Long ago the Chinese found that a little bar of magnetic iron always pointed in the same direction if it were allowed to swing freely. Even a bar of ordinary iron-say, a small poker-will always come to rest pointing in the same direction if suspended by a string about its middle. But if the bar is also **magnetized**, it will come to rest much more quickly.

10   At first, the little "bar" or needle was floated on water, but men found it more useful to suspend it on a fine **pivot**, so that it could swing freely and easily. The Arabs borrowed the idea from the Chinese, and it was the Arabs who passed on the knowledge to Europeans.

(2)

      The compass needle, then, points always in the same direction. Why? It is
15   difficult to explain. Perhaps when you know more science, and learn more about the laws obeyed by magnets, you will begin to understand why a **magnetic needle** always points to the same spot on the earth's surface.

      Simple exercises may now be devised to prove that a magnetized needle always
20   comes to rest pointing in the same direction. Any number of needles may be sufficiently magnetized by rubbing them on a large bar or horseshoe magnet. Children may then experiment with their
25   needles both at school and at home. They will discover the advantage of the pivoted over the **floated needle**, and the value of marking the north-pointing end. It is now easy to understand the value of the **compass card** which rides on the back of the needle, and is carried by it in its
30   swing.

(3)

      The teacher, of course, has for school use a large **mariner's compass**, which readily takes to pieces to show the parts. He shows the needle (from which the card has been removed) and the pivot on which it swings. He allows it to come to rest side by side with a magnetized needle floating in a basin of water. Both

35

point in the same direction. He next fixes a **blank** circular card on the needle's back, and shows the advantage of it by marking on it the **cardinal** points, which children will readily give him.

40   How to construct a simple compass card? On a card let children draw a large circle, and through its center two diameters at **right angles** to each other. Name the points N., S., E., W. A few exercises will show that these four alone are very **inadequate**. Insert N.E., N.W., S.E., S.W., by drawing thinner **diameters** midway between each pair of those already drawn.

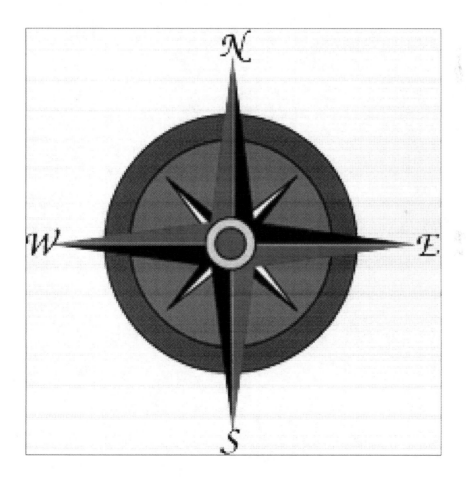

Reading Comprehension

Exercise 1	Part 1

Read Part 1 silently, and then answer these questions.

1. What helps man to find direction?

    _____

2. Does an iron bar show direction?

    _____

3. Which shows direction more quickly: an iron bar or a magnetized one?

    _____

4. What is the structure of a modern compass?

    _____

5. Who initiated the idea of the compass?

    _____

Exercise 2	Part 2

Read Part 2 silently, and then answer these questions.

1. How can we magnetize an iron bar?

    _____

2. Which is better: a floating needle or a pivoted one?

    _____

3. Where does the magnetic needle point?

    _____

4. What law does the magnetic needle obey?

    _____

Listening Comprehension

Exercise 3	Part 3

Close your book, and listen to your instructor reading   Part 3. Then answer these questions.

1. What does the needle swing on?

_____

2. Who needs the compass most?

_____

3. Why does the mariner need the compass very urgently?

_____

4. What do N, S, E, W stand for?

_____

5. What do NE, NW, SE, and SW stand for?

_____

Vocabulary

Exercise 4	Word Matching

Match the words of similar meanings in both lists.

List A   List B

1. sufficiently   _____   **a.** mariner

2. happen   _____   **b.** occur

3. foggy   _____   **c.** comprehend

4. suspend   _____   **d.** enough

5. sailor   _____   **e.** misty

6. understand   _____   **f.** diameter

                                                               g. hang

Exercise 5	Adjective Derivation

Derive adjectives from these words.

1. science   _____   **6.** fix   _____

2. magnet   _____   **7.** circle   _____

3. easily   _____   **8.** value   _____

4. instrument   _____   **9.** suffice   _____

5. experiment   _____   **10.** center   _____

Exercise 6	Double Roles

Use each word as a noun and as a verb.

1. water   a. _____

          b. _____

2. point   a. _____

          b. _____

3. circle   a. _____

          b. _____

4. exercise   a. _____

          b. _____

5. school   a. _____

          b. _____

Grammar

| Exercise 7 | Prepositions |

> Notice that hours take **at**, days take **on**, and months and years take **in**, e.g., **at** 7 o'clock, **on** Sunday, **in** March, **in** 2003.

Add the suitable preposition in each blank.

1. He will arrive _____ 3 o'clock _____the afternoon
    _____ Monday.

2. A compass uses a bar _____ magnetic iron.

3. A compass needle always points _____ the same direction.

4. The needle may float _____ water.

5. They borrowed the idea _____ another nation.

6. You need to learn more _____ science.

7. He was born _____ September.

8. The Second World War started _____ 1939.

| Exercise 8 | Present Perfect Continuous |

> The present perfect continuous tense consists of "**have**" or "**has**" + **been** + the **present participle**, e.g., have been writing.

Change these verbs into the present perfect continuous tense.

1. They lived in Greece for twelve years.

_____

2.   He taught at the school for five years.

_____

3.   He learned English for ten years.

_____

4.   The scientist has conducted research on cancer since 1995.

_____

5.   The students waited for the bus for two hours.

_____

Exercise 9	Since and For

> We use **since** before a point of time, but we use **for** before a duration of time, e.g., **since** Sunday, **for** three days.

Add since **or** for **in the blanks.**

1.   I haven't seen him _____ two years.

2.   He hasn't come home _____ 2000.

3.   He has been waiting here _____ noon.

4.   They have been swimming _____ three hours.

5.   He has been awake _____ midnight.

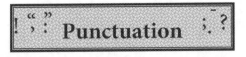

Punctuation

Exercise 10	Mark Addition

Add capital letters, full stops, and question marks wherever necessary.

1. where does mr smith live

    _____

2. have you seen the ruins of petra

    _____

3. have you read hamlet

    _____

4. do you know turkish or greek

    _____

5. i have no idea about this matter

    _____

ABCDEFGHI
JKLMN   **Spelling and Dictation**   *OPQRSTUV*
                                                        WXYZ

Exercise 11 | **Apostrophe**

> We add *'s* after singular nouns like **man's** and after irregular plurals like **women's**. We usually add *'* after singular proper nouns ending in *s* and after regular plurals, e.g., *Jesus', farmers'*.

Paraphrase these structures using 's or '.

1. the books of the boys   _____

2. the car of the student   _____

3. the hats of the men   _____

4. the bags of the children   _____

5. the house of Moses   _____

Exercise 12	Practice

Practice the spelling of these words.

1. sufficient	_____	10. needle	_____
2. diameter	_____	11. compass	_____
3. inadequate	_____	12. Chinese	_____
4. magnetized	_____	13. knowledge	_____
5. science	_____	14. European	_____
6. borrow	_____	15. horseshoe	_____
7. suspend	_____	16. float	_____
8. exercise	_____	17. value	_____
9. advantage	_____	18. angle	_____

Exercise 13	Dictation

You may have any paragraph in the passage or a part of it as a dictation exercise, depending on your instructor's choice.

_____

_____

_____

_____

☐ Pronunciation ☐

Exercise 14	Past Endings

> *Regular verbs, i.e., verbs with -ed in Form 2 and Form 3, have three phonetic endings: /ɪd/, /t/, and /d/, e.g., commanded, noticed, and moved, respectively.*

Pronounce these past verbs. Notice the differences between the three groups:
/id/, /t/, or /d/; *each column here makes a group. Fill in each blank with the right ending.*

1. needed _____   5. kicked _____   9. roamed _____

2. demanded _____   6. jumped _____   10. played _____

3. wanted _____   7. Picked _____   11. judged _____

4. requested _____   8. brushed _____   12. happened _____

Exercise 15   **Stress**

Pronounce and re-write these words, putting the strong stress on the right syllable, e.g., táble.

1. landmark _____   6. surface _____

2. direction _____   7. needle _____

3. suspend _____   8. discover _____

4. always _____   9. understand _____

5. magnetic _____   10. compass _____

Free Writing

Exercise 16   **Paragraph Writing**

Write a ten-line paragraph on the structure and use of the compass.

_____

_____

Unit 3

SOLIDS, LIQUIDS,
AND GASES

(1)

Most people would describe water as a colorless liquid. They would know that in very cold conditions it becomes a solid called **ice,** and that when heated on a fire it becomes a vapor called **steam**. But water, they would say, is a **liquid**.

We have learned that water consists of **molecules** composed of two atoms of hydrogen and one atom of oxygen, which we describe by the **formula** H_2O. But this is equally true of the solid called ice and the gas called steam. Chemically, there is no difference between the gas, the liquid, and the solid, all of which are made up of molecules with the formula H_2O. And this is true of other **chemical substances;** most of them can exist

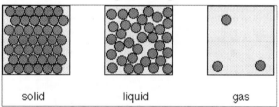

as gases or as liquids or as solids. We may normally think of iron as a solid, but if we heat it in a furnace it will melt and become a liquid, and at very high temperatures it will become a gas. We normally think of air as a mixture of gases, but at very low **temperatures** it becomes a liquid, and at lower temperatures still it becomes a white solid.

(2)

Nothing very permanent occurs when a gas changes into a liquid or a solid. Everyone knows that ice, which has been made by freezing water, can be melted again by being warmed; and that steam can be **condensed** on a cold surface to become **liquid water**. In

25   fact, it is only because water is such a familiar substance that different

names are used for the solid, liquid, and
gas. For other substances we have to
describe these different states directly.
Thus, for air we talk about liquid air and

30   solid air. We could also talk about
gaseous air, but since this is the normal
thing, we usually just describe it as air.

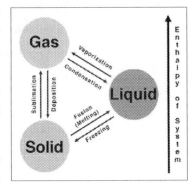

What, then, do we mean when we
say that water is a liquid, air is a gas, and

35   salt is a solid? We mean nothing more than that this is the usual condition
of things on our earth. On one of the **outer planets** all three substances
would be solids, and on the sun all three would be gases. Most substances
are only familiar to us in one state, because the temperatures required to
turn them into gases are very high, or the temperatures necessary to turn

40   them into solids are so low. Water is an **exception** in this respect, which is
another reason why its three states have been given three different names.

(3)

The fact that a liquid like water
can be changed to solid ice and back
again to water, just by changing the

45   temperature, would lead us to suppose
that the very strong **bonds** between the
atoms in the H_2O molecules have not

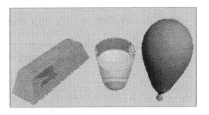

been greatly changed, and the examination of water, ice, and steam shows
that this is true, and that all of them consist of H_2O molecules. The

50   difference between these three different forms of water lies simply in the
arrangement of the H_2O molecules or their **position** with respect to each
other.

Reading Comprehension

Exercise 1 | **Part 1**

Read Part 1 silently, and then answer these questions.

1. What color is water?

_____

2. What are the three forms of water?

_____

3. What is the chemical formula of water?

_____

4. When does iron change into a liquid?

_____

5. Can iron become a gas?

_____

Exercise 2 | **Part 2**

Read Part 2 silently, and then answer these questions.

1. What material results from freezing water?

_____

2. What material results from melting ice?

_____

3. What material results from condensing steam?

_____

4. Why do we say water is a liquid when it can be a solid or a gas?

_____

5. How is water exceptional?

_____

Listening Comprehension

Exercise 3	Part 3

Close your book, and listen to your instructor reading   Part 3. Then answer these questions.

1. What is the formula of water as a liquid?

    _____

2. How can water be changed to solid ice?

    _____

3. What is the formula of water as steam?

    _____

4. What is the difference between the three forms of water?

Vocabulary

Exercise 4	Adjective Derivation

> *Some suffixes mark adjectives and are thus called* **adjective-forming suffixes**, *e.g., -less, -ful, -ic, -ive, -ary, -ous, -y, -al.*

Derive adjectives from these words.

1. color   _____   6. normally   _____

2. ice   _____   7. exception   _____

3. atom   _____   8. planet   _____

4. gas   _____   9. describe   _____

5. molecule   _____   10. whiteness   _____

Exercise 5 | The Suffix -less

Every prefix or suffix has a meaning. The suffix -*less* means "without". This suffix is usually added to nouns to make adjectives, e.g., care*less*.

Form new adjectives by adding -less to these nouns.

1. water _____   6. harm _____

2. plant _____   7. rain _____

3. color _____   8. ice _____

4. gas _____   9. noise _____

5. use _____   10. home _____

Exercise 6 | Word Production

Give one word for each phrase; the first letter is given to help you produce the answer.

1. Having no color: c_____

2. The solid form of water: i_____

3. The gas form of water: s_____

4. A group of atoms: m_____

5. Turning steam into water: c_____

Grammar

Exercise 7 | Prepositions

Add the suitable preposition in each blank.

1. Water consists _____ hydrogen and oxygen.

2. We describe water _____ the formula H_2O.

3. This fact is true _____ all substances.

4. There is no chemical difference _____ all the forms of water.

5. A gas can be changed _____ a liquid.

6. A solid can be a liquid _____ a very high temperature.

7. Let's talk _____ this matter later.

8. He is a familiar face _____ me.

Exercise 8	Relative Omission

> The **relative pronoun** *may be omitted if it is not the subject of the relative clause provided that it is not preceded by a preposition, e.g., This is the book* (which) *I bought yesterday.*

Omit the relative pronoun if possible, and re-write the sentence after this omission.

1. The film *which* we saw last night was very useful.

    _____

2. The music to *which* we listened last night was nice.

    _____

3. The students for *whom* he was waiting were late.

    _____

4. I returned the money *that* I had borrowed from my friend.

    _____

5. I thanked the man *who* helped me.

    _____

Exercise 9 | so ... that

> The structure **so... that** is used to express the result, e.g., He studied **so** hard **that** most of his grades were above 85.

Combine each pair of sentences into one sentence, using *so ... that.*

1. The tea was very hot. I couldn't drink it.
_____

2. The lesson was very difficult. I couldn't understand it.
_____

3. The food was very salty. I couldn't eat it.
_____

4. The river was very deep. I couldn't cross it.
_____

5. The mountain was very steep. I couldn't climb it.
_____

Punctuation

Exercise 10 | Stops and Commas

Add a comma or a full stop where necessary.

1. Hani is a good student
_____

2. Hani Wisam and Muneer are good students
_____

3. Majdi one of my friends has just left for Beirut
_____

4. Do you understand what I'm saying John?

    _____

5. Yes I do

    _____

ABCDEFGHI JKLMN	**Spelling and Dictation**	OPQRSTUV WXYZ

Exercise 11	***Self* Forms**

> Notice that **self forms** are written as one word each, not two, e.g., *ourselves*.

Combine these two units into one word, making any necessary changes.

1. I + self   _____   5. it + self   _____

2. you + self   _____   6. they + self   _____

3. she + self   _____   7. we + self   _____

4. he + self   _____   8. you + self   _____

Exercise 12	**Practice**

Practice the spelling of these words.

1. condition   _____   6. gaseous   _____

2. molecule   _____   7. temperature   _____

3. formula   _____   8. oxygen   _____

4. condense   _____   9. hydrogen   _____

5. exception   _____   10. chemical   _____

Exercise 13	Dictation

You may have any paragraph in the passage or a part of it as a dictation exercise, depending on your instructor's choice.

_____

_____

_____

_____

_____

Pronunciation

Exercise 14	Silent h

> If **wh-** comes initially, **h** is usually silent, e.g., when.

Pronounce these words, noticing the silent h after w. Re-write each word putting a dot under any silent letter.

1. when   _____   6. wheat   _____

2. where   _____   7. wheel   _____

3. why   _____   8. whether   _____

4. what   _____   9. which   _____

5. whale   _____   10. whip   _____

Exercise 15	Stress

Pronounce and re-write these words, putting the strong stress on the right syllable, e.g., fúrnace.

1. compose	_____	6. arrangement	_____
2. oxygen	_____	7. familiar	_____
3. describe	_____	8. condition	_____
4. substance	_____	9. normal	_____
5. examination	_____	10. difference	_____

✍ Free Writing ✍

Exercise 16	Précis

Summarize all the passage in a paragraph of about ten lines.

_____

_____

_____

_____

_____

_____

_____

_____

_____

_____

Unit 4

LANGUAGE AND COMMUNITY

(1)

The speakers of any language do not speak their language in the same way. They are naturally affected by geographical, economic, cultural, and **social factors**. In addition, there are differences among individual speakers caused by the factors of age, sex, education, and profession. As a result of this complicated **net of factors,** a very wide variety of dialects come into being. These dialects are discussed under a branch of linguistics called **sociolinguistics**.

As people speaking the same language spread over a wide geographical area, **dialectal differences** among them increase. The larger the geographical distance between two groups of the same language community is, the greater the **inter-dialectal differences** will be. Dialects that characterize certain regions are called regional or **geographical dialects**.

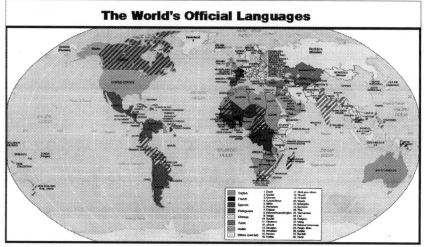

The World's Official Languages

(2)

These **regional dialects** are caused and enhanced by a variety of reasons. First, different regions have different **language contacts** determined by bordering foreign communities. The border contacts of the English people, for example, differ from the **border contacts** of Americans, Australians, or Canadians. That is partly why each nation has a distinct dialect. Second, if a group of people is geographically isolated behind a natural barrier such as mountains, deserts, and oceans or by a **political barrier**, this situation will intensify **dialectal differences** between isolated groups.

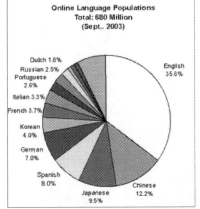

In fact, every language has its own main geographical dialects. Every main dialect, furthermore, develops into minor sub-dialects. For instance, English has the variety of British English, American English, Black English, Arab English, Indian English, and many others. American English, for example, has the eastern dialect, the midland dialect, and the western dialect. Each of these three dialects has **sub-dialects** that keep on narrowing down until they reach the **town-dialect** level.

(3)

People differ as to their social, economic, and **educational status**. Such factors certainly influence the person's dialect. If you listen well, you can easily see the difference between an educated man's dialect and an **illiterate** man's dialect. A professor's dialect is surely different from a miner's dialect. The speaker's educational level is a **basic factor** here, resulting in the determination of the level and type of social companionship. Who you are determines with whom you socialize. So do your economic status and social status. People belonging to the same socio-economic group tend to form a distinct **social dialect** simply because they differ from other social groups.

Let us assume that two individuals belong to the same region, live in the same city and even the same street, belong to the same family, and have the same **socio-economic** status. Nevertheless, their **individual dialects** will inevitably be different.

Everyone speaks his native or foreign language in a unique manner that distinguishes him from any other speaker. This unique manner is called an **idiolect**. A language like English spoken natively by about 500 million people has, in fact, about 500 million distinct idiolects. No two persons speak a certain language in exactly the same way.

Reading Comprehension

| Exercise 1 | Part 1 |

Read Part 1 silently, and then answer these questions.

1. Do the speakers of Arabic speak Arabic in the same way?

2. What branch of linguistics studies dialects?

3. Does a wider distance between two regions cause more differences between dialects or less?

4. What do we call dialects in different countries speaking the same language?

| Exercise 2 | Part 2 |

Read Part 2 silently, and then answer these questions.

1. Does a desert separating two regions increase or decrease differences between dialects?

2. Give some examples of regional dialects of English.

3. Are there dialects within the same dialect?

4. What are dialects within a dialect called?

Listening Comprehension

Exercise 3 | Part 3

Close your book, and listen to your instructor reading   Part 3. Then answer these questions.

1. Does the individual's education affect his dialect?

   _____

2. Does the economic status of the individual affect his dialect?

   _____

3. What do we call the dialect produced by the economic and educational level?

   _____

4. What is an idiolect?

   _____

Vocabulary

Exercise 4 | Word Matching

Match words of similar meanings in the two lists.

List A		List B
1. isolated	_____	a. geographical
2. distinct	_____	b. closed
3. regional	_____	c. mix
4. blocked	_____	d. quite different
5. socialize	_____	e. suppose

6. assume   _____   **f.** separated

7. inevitable   _____   **g.** unavoidable

                                                 h. nevertheless

Exercise 5	Affix Meaning

> *Notice that **-er** has three meanings: "doer" as in "teacher", "more" as in "larger", and "who belongs to" as in "Londoner".*

Give the meanings of the underlined affixes.

1. speak<u>er</u>   _____   6. Canad<u>ian</u>   _____

2. cultur<u>al</u>   _____   7. intens<u>ify</u>   _____

3. dialect<u>s</u>   _____   8. <u>sub</u>-dialect   _____

4. great<u>er</u>   _____   9. differ<u>ence</u>   _____

5. <u>inter</u>-dialectal   _____   10. character<u>ize</u>   _____

Exercise 6	Word Comparison

Compare the words of each pair, using each in a sentence.

1. **a.** minor   _____
    b. miner   _____

2. **a.** economic   _____
    b. economics _____

3. **a.** desert   _____
    b. dessert   _____

4. **a.** status   _____
    b. states   _____

5. **a.** result in _____
    b. result from _____

Grammar

Exercise 7 | neither ... nor

English has four paired or correlative conjunctions: **either... or, neither... nor, both... and, not only... but also**.

Combine each pair of sentences into one sentence using neither ... nor.

1. He does not know French. He does not know German.

    _____

2. She doesn't have a pen. He doesn't have a pencil.

    _____

3. Hani hasn't come yet. Majdi hasn't come yet.

    _____

4. She doesn't like to play. He doesn't like to swim.

    _____

5. Don't lend them money. Don't borrow money from them.

    _____

Exercise 8 | either ... or

Combine each pair of sentences into one sentence using either ... or.

1. You may speak English at the conference. You may speak Arabic.

    _____

2.   You may use a pen. You may use a pencil.

   _____

3.   He will fly to Rome. He will fly to Paris.

   _____

4.   He will specialize in physics. He will specialize in chemistry.

   _____

5.   The child will live with his mother. The child will live with his grandmother.

   _____

Exercise 9	the ... the

> *The conditional sentence can be replaced by a* **the-the structure,** *where each* **the** *is followed by a comparative word. If you study harder, your grades will be higher* ⟹ **The** *harder you study,* **the** *higher your grades will be.*

Paraphrase each sentence using the ... the.

1.   If you practice English more, you become more fluent.

   _____

2.   If you do it sooner, it will be better.

   _____

3.   If the demand is more, prices will be higher.

   _____

4.   If the supply is less, prices will go higher.

   _____

5.   If he is older, he will get wiser.

   _____

Punctuation

Exercise 10   Mark Addition

> Notice that the **exclamation mark** (!) is used at the end of exclamatory sentences, requests, and commands.

Add the capital letter, full stop, question mark, and exclamation mark wherever necessary.

1. what a beautiful day it is

    _____

2. what is the cost of this project

    _____

3. how wonderful this garden is

    _____

4. stop making noise, please

    _____

5. don't forget the orders

    _____

6. how far is it

    _____

7. how far it is

    _____

ABCDEFGHI JKLMN   Spelling and Dictation   OPQRSTUV WXYZ

Exercise 11   One Word

Re-write these units as one word or more, as required.

1. never+the+less _____
2. more+over _____
3. in+addition _____
4. there+fore _____
5. for+ever _____

6. with+out _____
7. of+course _____
8. what+ever _____
9. now+adays _____
10. them+selves _____

| Exercise 12 | Practice |

Practice the spelling of these words.

1. dialect _____
2. idiolect _____
3. sub-dialect _____
4. regional _____
5. socio-economic _____

6. cultural _____
7. geographical _____
8. inevitably _____
9. intensify _____
10. identify _____

| Exercise 13 | Dictation |

You may have any paragraph in the passage or a part of it as a dictation exercise, depending on your instructor's choice.

_____
_____
_____
_____
_____
_____
_____

Pronunciation

Exercise 14	Plural Suffix

The plural suffix can be pronounced /ɨz/, /s/, or /z/, depending on the final sound of the singular, e.g., brushes, books, dogs, respectively.

Pronounce these plural nouns. Is the final /ɨz/, /s/, or /z/?

1. buses   _____   7. looks   _____

2. passages   _____   8. pets   _____

3. watches   _____   9. doors   _____

4. churches   _____   10. days   _____

5. kites   _____   11. robes   _____

6. books   _____   12. trees   _____

Exercise 15	Stress

Pronounce and re-write these words, putting the strong stress on the right syllable, e.g., Canádian.

1. Australian   _____   6. influence   _____

2. factor   _____   7. develop   _____

3. dialect   _____   8. individual   _____

4. resulting   _____   9. economic   _____

5. determine   _____   10. desert   _____

Free Writing

Exercise 16	Précis

Summarize the passage of this unit in a ten-line paragraph.

_____

_____

_____

_____

_____

_____

_____

_____

_____

_____

Unit 5

WEIGHT AND MASS

(1)

What is weight? Why is it easier to ride a bicycle along a flat road than to ride it up a hill? Why is it possible to free-wheel downhill on a bicycle without **pedalling** at all? To answer these questions, we need to find out something about weight. Try some simple **experiments** with a stone. Hold the stone out in front of your face, and let it go; it will fall to the ground. Take the stone outside, and throw it straight forward, **parallel** to the ground, as strongly as you can. It will move rapidly away from you, but as it moves forward it will also be falling. If you watch a stone thrown in this way by someone else, you will see that its path is a **downward curve**.

Take the stone again, and throw it straight up into the air. It will move upwards very quickly at first, and then more and more slowly, until, for an **instant**, it is not moving at all. Then it will move downwards again, falling more and more quickly until it strikes the  ground. In each experiment, we can see by the movement of the stone that it is being drawn downward towards the earth, almost as if a string were tied to it; this earthward pull is called the **force of gravity**. Now pick the stone up and let it **rest** in your fingers . You can feel that the downward force is still **acting**, even though the stone is held at rest. If it is to be stopped from moving downwards, it is necessary to **push** or **pull** it upwards, with a force which acts in the opposite way to the force of gravity. The downward force of gravity on a body is called the **weight** of the body. The upward force of your fingers is called the **reaction** of your fingers to the weight of the stone.

It is the weight of the bicycle and its **rider** which makes it possible to ride downhill without pedalling. All bodies on or near the earth have weight, **that is**, they are being pulled downwards towards the earth.

(2)

Weight is not the same everywhere. Weight is a pull caused by the earth. **Consequently**, if the earth were taken away, all weight would disappear. In outer space, far from the earth or from any other attracting body, objects are almost **weightless**. On the moon, objects have less weight than they have on the earth, because the moon is less heavy than the earth and pulls downward less strongly. In the last **decade**, men have been able to perform experiments on **weightlessness**. You will have read in newspapers and books about the space-rockets and satellites, bodies which can be projected far out of the earth's atmosphere into space. When a 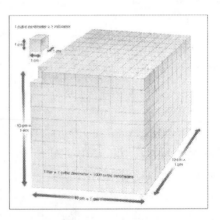 space-rocket or satellite is floating freely, with its rocket engines switched off, bodies inside it are, effectively, weightless. The strange effect produced is shown by some experiments. These mice are in a **free-floating satellite**, and they, therefore, have no weight. There is no force pulling them 'downwards' or 'upwards'; they have no sense of 'up' and 'down' because this sense depends on gravity. They float about freely in any **position**. A light **tap** on one wall will send them drifting across to the opposite wall, and they can hold on to the 'ceiling' of the satellite just as easily as on to the 'floor'. There are now many people who have experienced weightlessness for themselves. **Astronauts** who undertake **space flights** are trained to **endure** weightlessness, and have described in detail what it feels like to be without weight.

(3)

Mass is the same everywhere. In a space-rocket floating freely, men have no **effective weight**. But the men still exist; they are still as solid as they were on earth, and if they bump their heads together as they are floating around inside the rocket, the bump is just as painful as it would be on earth. The men are unchanged; the weightlessness is caused by a change in the forces acting on them, and not by any change in the men themselves. To express this briefly, the word mass is used. We say that the men are as massive in the **space-ship** as they were when they were on earth. Their weight has become zero, because they have moved into a **region** where **gravity** cannot act, but their mass is unchanged.

Reading Comprehension

Exercise 1	Part 1

Read Part 1 silently, and then answer these questions.

1.   Which is easier: to ride a bicycle along a flat road or up a hill? Why?

2.   If you hold a stone and let it go, where will it go?

3.   If you throw a stone straight forward, how will it go?

4.   If you throw a stone upward, what happens to its movement?

5.   What pulls things downward?

Exercise 2	Part 2

Read Part 2 silently, and then answer these questions.

1.   Which is heavier: something on the earth or on the moon?

2.   What is your weight in outer space?

3.   What is the reason for weightlessness?

4.   Do weightless persons in space have a sense of 'up' or 'down'?

Listening Comprehension

Exercise 3	Part 3

Close your book, and listen to your instructor reading   Part 3. Then answer these questions.

1. In a space rocket, do men have weight?

    _____

2. In a space rocket, do men have mass?

    _____

3. Which is changeable: mass or weight?

    _____

4. If something has no weight, does it exist?

    _____

5. If something has no mass, does it exist?

    _____

Vocabulary

Exercise 4	Part 4

Give the opposite of each following word.

1. downward   _____   6. experienced   _____

2. forward   _____   7. effective   _____

3. possible   _____   8. brief   _____

4. up   _____   9. painful   _____

5. changeable   _____   10. slow   _____

Exercise 5	Noun Derivation

> Some suffixes are **noun-forming suffixes**, i.e., used to form nouns. Examples are **-ness, -ity, -ion, -ence, -th, -ment**.

Derive nouns from these adjectives by adding the suitable suffix.

1. flat	_____		6. strong	_____
2. weightless	_____		7. effective	_____
3. necessary	_____		8. brief	_____
4. consequent	_____		9. dependent	_____
5. heavy	_____		10. slow	_____

Exercise 6	Affix Meaning

> Remember that every prefix or suffix has a meaning, e.g., **tri-** (=three), **-ity** (=state of being).

What is the meaning of the underlined unit?

1. <u>bi</u>cycle	_____		5. react<u>ion</u>	_____
2. strong<u>ly</u>	_____		6. <u>dis</u>appear	_____
3. down<u>ward</u>	_____		7. weight<u>less</u>	_____
4. stopp<u>ed</u>	_____		8. weightless<u>ness</u>	_____

Grammar

Exercise 7	Verbs and Tenses

> Verbs in English can be in **twelve tenses**. **Past tenses** can be past simple, past perfect, past continuous, or past perfect continuous. So-can be **present tenses** and **future tenses**.

Re-read the last paragraph in Part 3, underline the verb of every sentence, and mention its tense. Make a list of the first eight verbs and their tenses here.

Verb	Tense	Verb	Tense

Exercise 8 | **can = be able to**

The auxiliary "**can**" indicates "**ability**" in the present or future. It may be replaced by one of these: **is able to, am able to, are able to, will be able to.**

Change can **into** be able to **or** will be able to.

1. You can do it right now.

   _____

2. She can see him tomorrow.

   _____

3. You can learn a foreign language in one year.

   _____

4. He can pass the test if he studies hard enough.

   _____

5. They can improve their fitness by more physical exercises.

   _____

Exercise 9 | **Noun Clauses**

A noun clause usually begins with one of these: **wh-word, that, how, whether,** or **if.**

Fill in the blanks with a word of these: what, when, which, that, whether, why, where.

1. _____ the earth is spherical is a fact.

2. _____ you say needs to be proved.

3. _____ he lives now is not known by his parents.

4. _____ he was born is a questionable date.

5. _____ he will come tomorrow or not waits to be seen.

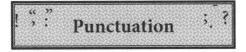

Exercise 10	Mark Addition

Add a capital letter, comma, or full stop where necessary.

1. he said "i will do it now"

_____

2. she read the poem did the exercise and wrote the assignment

_____

3. ali my friend has not arrived yet

_____

4. john come here

_____

5. they are good students aren't they?

_____

6. if you see him tell him

_____

ABCDEFGHI JKLMN Spelling and Dictation OPQRSTUV WXYZ

Exercise 11 | One Word

*These pronouns are written as one word: **anyone, anybody, anything, none, nobody, nothing, someone, somebody, something, everyone, everybody, everything**. They are called **indefinite pronouns**.*

Are these written as one word or more? Re-write them in the correct form.

1. my + self   _____

6. some + time   _____

2. in + spite + of   _____

7. some + times   _____

3. any + thing   _____

8. every + one   _____

4. any + time   _____

9. every + day   _____

5. any + day   _____

10. some + things   _____

Exercise 12 | Practice

Practice the spelling of these words.

1. upwards   _____

6. experience   _____

2. weight   _____

7. opposite   _____

3. gravity   _____

8. astronauts   _____

4. reaction   _____

9. perform   _____

5. experiment   _____

10. space-rocket _____

Exercise 13 | Dictation

You may have any paragraph in the passage or a part of it as a dictation exercise, depending on your instructor's choice.

Pronunciation

Exercise 14 | Similar Words

> Words pronounced the same way with different meanings are called **homophones**, *e.g., I, eye.*

Are these pairs pronounced exactly the same (S) or differently (D)?Write S or D in the blanks.

1. she's, cheese   _____

2. chose, choose   _____

3. juice, Jews   _____

4. shows, shoes   _____

5. rid, red   _____

6. could, good   _____

7. bear, bare   _____

8. ate, eight   _____

9. mist, missed   _____

10. whose, hose   _____

Exercise 15 | Stress

Say and re-write these words marking the strong stress on the right syllable, e.g., grávity.

1. endure   _____

2. weightless   _____

6. opposite   _____

7. decade   _____

3. themselves	_____	8. attracting	_____
4. unchanged	_____	9. experiment	_____
5. satellite	_____	10. newspapers	_____

Free Writing

Exercise 16 — Précis

Summarize all the passage of this unit in a paragraph of about ten lines.

_____

_____

_____

_____

_____

_____

_____

_____

_____

_____

Unit 6

SPEECH ORGANS

(1)

One characteristic that distinguishes man from animals is his ability to produce **speech sounds**, i.e., language sounds. This characteristic is made possible by three factors: man's nature as created by God, man's **mental ability** that enables him to learn and innovate, and man's **articulation organs** that make speech possible. It is interesting to notice that speech organs are not created solely for speech; they have other functions as well. The nose and the mouth, for example, are **breath passages**; the teeth and the tongue have essential roles in food chewing. Most **speech organs**, if not all, have breathing, eating, or drinking as their primary function. Speech comes as an additional or secondary function of the so-called speech organs.

(2)

The human **speech system** consists of many speech organs, most of which are in the chest, throat, and head. These organs will be explained in the following paragraphs.

Abdominal muscles play an essential role in speech articulation through relaxation and contraction, the two processes which help raise and lower the diaphragm, a membrane which separates the chest from the **abdomen**. When the diaphragm rises, it presses the lungs upward, assisting **exhalation**. When the diaphragm goes down, it causes the lungs to relax making room for **inhalation**. Notice that speech is essentially dependent on inhalation and exhalation, since there is no speech without exhalation, which cannot happen without inhalation.

Above the abdomen, and between it and the chest, there is a membrane called the **diaphragm**. This diaphragm helps the lungs to **contract** upon
25 exhalation and to relax upon inhalation. Notice that speech usually happens during exhalation.

(3)

Above the diaphragm there are the two lungs, which are the source of the **breath stream**, which is pushed out during exhalation and is made to pass through the throat and then through the mouth or the nose freely or semi-freely,producing a

30

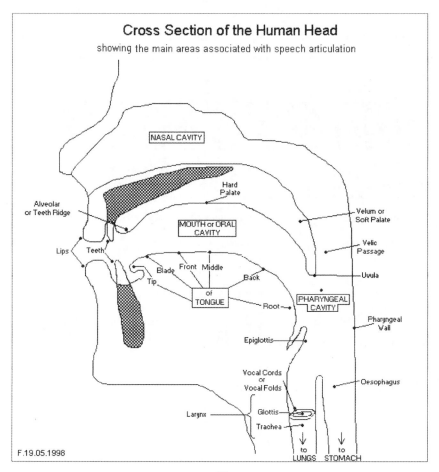

Cross Section of the Human Head
showing the main areas associated with speech articulation

NASAL CAVITY

Hard Palate

Alveolar or Teeth Ridge

Velum or Soft Palate

MOUTH or ORAL CAVITY

Velic Passage

Lips   Teeth

Blade Front Middle
Tip   Back

Uvula

of
TONGUE

Root

PHARYNGEAL CAVITY

Pharyngeal Wall

Epiglottis

Vocal Cords
or
Vocal Folds

Oesophagus

Larynx

Glottis

Trachea

to   to
LUNGS   STOMACH

F.19.05.1998

variety of speech sounds. The two lungs are the **source of energy**, without which no speech can occur.

Around the two lungs there are **chest muscles**, sometimes called **intercostal muscles**, which control the size of the chest cavity through their
35   contraction and relaxation. With longer contraction, exhalation extends longer in time. This results in a longer **speech group**. Since there is no speech without exhalation, the longer exhalation is, the longer speech continues. When exhalation ends, speech ends too, and inhalation takes place again, followed by **re-exhalation** in a continuous process repeated along one's entire
40   life.

Other important speech organs are the **windpipe**, larynx with its **vocal cords**, pharynx, i.e., throat, tongue, lower lip, upper lip, teeth, palate, mouth, and   nose.

Reading Comprehension

Exercise 1   Part 1

Read Part 1 silently, and then answer these questions.

1.   Can animals produce speech sounds?

_____

2.   Is there a difference between speech organs and articulation organs?

_____

3.   Is speech the only function of speech organs?

_____

4.   What is the main function of the nose?

_____

5. What is the main function of teeth?

_____

Exercise 2	Part 2

Read Part 2 silently, and then answer these questions.

1. Where are speech organs located?

_____

2. What is the membrane between the chest and the abdomen?

_____

3. When the diaphragm rises up, does it help exhalation or inhalation?

_____

4. When does speech happen: during exhalation or during inhalation?

_____

5. Do abdominal muscles have a direct role in speech or an indirect one?

_____

Listening Comprehension

Exercise 3	Part 3

Close your book, and listen to your instructor reading   Part 3. Then answer these questions.

1. What is the source of the breath stream?

_____

2.   What is the breath passage after the throat?

   _____

3.   What happens when chest muscles contract: exhalation or inhalation?

   _____

4.   Does long exhalation make speech shorter or longer?

   _____

5.   Can there be exhalation without inhalation?

   _____

Vocabulary

Exercise 4 | Noun Derivation

Derive nouns from these words.

1. exhale   _____   6. speak   _____

2. inhale   _____   7. possible   _____

3. distinguish   _____   8. contract   _____

4. create   _____   9. separate   _____

5. articulate   _____   10. relax   _____

Exercise 5 | Word Selection

Add the missing word choosing one of these words: mouth, exhalation, intercostal, abdomen, inhalation, nose, diaphragm.

1.   Every _____ process is followed by exhalation.

2.   Chest muscles are also called _____ muscles.

3.   The _____ is a membrane between the _____ and the chest.

4.   Speech occurs during _____.

5.   The breath stream goes outside the body through the _____ or the _____.

Exercise 6	Word Matching

Match words of similar meanings in the two lists.

List A		List B
1. produce	_____	**a.** help
2. solely	_____	**b.** only
3. function	_____	**c.** happen
4. assist	_____	**d.** role
5. occur	_____	**e.** articulate
		f. repeat
		g. energy

Grammar

Exercise 7	Subject-Verb Agreement

*The subject and the verb must agree in number. This is called **subject-verb agreement**, e.g., he is, they are.*

Choose the right verb.

1.   Most of the book (is, are) easy.

2.   Most of the books (is, are) interesting.

_____

3.   Growing flowers (was, were) her hobby.

_____

4.   Politics (is, are) a good subject to specialize in.

_____

5.   He and she (speak, speaks) English very well.

_____

6.   You or I (am, are) the one who must do it.

_____

7.   Most people (like, likes) picnics.

_____

8.   Economics (is, are) an important subject.

_____

9.   None of the boys (is, are) here.

_____

10. The black and white bird (has, have) flown away.

_____

Exercise 8	only = none but

> The word **only** may be replaced by **none but** or **nothing but**: He knows only
> Arabic $\Longrightarrow$ He knows nothing but Arabic.

Paraphrase the sentence using *none but, no one but,* **or** *nothing but.*

1.   I know only Ali.

_____

2. He knows only French.

_____

3. He calls only his brother every week.

_____

4. He reads only five pages every day.

_____

5. He eats only vegetables and fruits.

_____

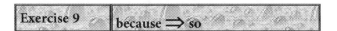

Exercise 9 | because ⟹ so

> The word **because** shows the reason, but the word **so** shows the result and takes a comma before it, e.g., He was sick, **so** he couldn't join the party.

Paraphrase the sentence using so, keeping the same meaning.

1. He didn't pass the test because he didn't prepare enough.

_____

2. He caught flue because he swam in very cold water.

_____

3. She missed the bus because she got up very late.

_____

4. They got sick because they did not wash the vegetables they ate yesterday.

_____

5. I didn't attend the meeting because I wasn't told about it.

_____

Punctuation

Exercise 10 · Commas

*If the relative clause is a **defining clause,** no commas are used, e.g., The book which I read yesterday is Ali's book. If it is a **non-defining clause,** commas are to be used before and after it, e.g., His father, who lives in Cairo, has arrived.*

Add commas in the squares where necessary.

1. Ali ☐ who is a close friend of mine ☐ knows everything about this matter.

2. The subject ☐ that was explained by the professor last week ☐ is very clear to me.

3. Amman ☐ which is the capital of Jordan ☐ is a very clean city.

4. Arabic ☐ which is the language of the Holy Quran ☐ is a very beautiful ☐ and expressive language.

5. His father ☐ who is about sixty ☐ always looks happy ☐ and healthy.

ABCDEFGHI JKLMN Spelling and Dictation OPQRSTUV WXYZ

Exercise 11 · Pluralization

*A word like "**country**" becomes "**countries**" in the plural, but a proper noun like "**Mary**" becomes "**Marys**".*

Give the plural of these nouns, observing correct spelling.

1. knife   _____   6. lady   _____

2. roof   _____   7. monkey   _____

3. mouse   _____   8. Vicky   _____

4. watch   _____   9. Nancy   _____

5. fairy   _____   10. sheep   _____

Exercise 12	Practice

Practice the spelling of these words.

1. characteristic   _____   6. diaphragm   _____

2. passage   _____   7. process   _____

3. additional   _____   8. exhalation   _____

4. system   _____   9. dependent   _____

5. energy   _____   10. relaxation   _____

Exercise 13	Dictation

You may have any paragraph in the passage or a part of it as a dictation exercise, depending on your instructor's choice.

_____

_____

_____

_____

Pronunciation

Exercise 14 | The Final *gn*

When **gn** is final, g is silent, e.g., sign.

Pronounce and re-write these words, putting a dot under g if it is silent.

1. sign   _____   6. foreign   _____

2. resign   _____   7. begin   _____

3. assign   _____   8. signature   _____

4. reign   _____   9. meaning   _____

5. sovereign   _____   10. resignation   _____

Exercise 15 | Stress

Pronounce and re-write these words, putting the strong stress on the right syllable, e.g., meáning.

1. distinguish   _____   6. extend   _____

2. notice   _____   7. exhalation   _____

3. passages   _____   8. cavity   _____

4. possible   _____   9. energy   _____

5. innovate   _____   10. articulation   _____

Free Writing

Exercise 16 | Paragraph Writing

Write a ten-line paragraph on speech organs.

_____

_____

_____

_____

_____

_____

_____

_____

_____

_____

Unit 7

MANAGER-EMPLOYEE RELATIONS

(1)

For three hundred years, there was a widespread totalitarian attitude on the part of supervisors: "Do it my way or you're fired." Since the 1960s, **manager-employee relations** have changed considerably and continue to change at a rapid rate. In today's **workplace**, there are certain employee rights
5 and freedoms supported to a great extent by state and federal laws as well as by special **interest groups**. These rights and freedoms cannot be sidestepped by the supervisor. They must be understood, seriously considered, and intelligently implemented.

10   The supervisor, the manager having the closest contact with the workers, is the individual most frequently confronted with the problem of dealing with changing attitudes of employees. The most likely area of confrontation is in alleged **discrimination**, where an employee feels that he or she is not being given fair consideration. When these **attitudinal**

15   **situations** occur, they must be quickly resolved, often by the first-level **supervisor**, to avoid their becoming agitations that spread to other employees and/or involve outside special interest groups. It is a real challenge to resolve attitudinal problems because the facts are so often "fuzzy" and the individuals involved are usually very emotional about the

20   situation.

(2)

    Another employee area undergoing significant change is *labor union-management relations*. **Inflation** with its resulting cost escalation, foreign competition, rising energy costs, greater demands for **quality control**, and decreasing worker productivity are bringing about attitudinal changes on

25   the part of both **labor leaders** and managers. The labor relations pendulum over a period of time has swung from the side of management to that

30   of **labor unions**. There are now many indicators that the gap between labor and management is closing. **Participative management** between the two groups appears to be more prevalent, with both sides making significant **concessions**.

(3)

35   A third factor affecting manager-employee relations is the changing composition of the work force. Women, older workers,

and **handicapped persons** are becoming more common in jobs once thought to
be inappropriate for them. Some are accepted by their **peers**, and some are not.

40   It is a challenge for the supervisor to effectively integrate these groups of workers
into a unified **work force**.

A major challenge for today's supervisors is to develop a more paternalistic
and **participative approach** to management problem solving and **decision
making**. In this area of management there is much to be learned from the

45   Japanese concept of quality control circles.

Reading Comprehension

Exercise 1	Part 1

*Read Part 1 silently, and then determine whether each statement is
true or false according to the text.*

1. Supervisors in the past were more democratic than supervisors of these
    days.

    _____

2. Employees now have more rights than before.

    _____

3. The supervisor has weak contact with the employees.

    _____

4. Employees rarely complain about unfair treatment.

    _____

5. When such complaints occur, they must be resolved by the supervisor
    at the top level.

    _____

Exercise 2	Part 2

Read Part 2 silently, and then answer these questions.

1. What is the area that has seen great change?

_____

2. Does inflation cause a decrease in costs? Why?

_____

3. What is the main goal of labor unions?

_____

4. What is the main goal of managers?

_____

5. What kind of management is prevailing now?

_____

Listening Comprehension

Exercise 3	Part 3

Close your book, and listen to your instructor reading   Part 3. Then answer these questions.

1. Does the work force now have more women or less?

_____

2. What is a handicapped person?

_____

3. What is the challenge for the manager now?

_____

4.   What is meant by a participative approach?

_____

5.   Can Japanese management be a good model to learn from?

_____

Vocabulary

Exercise 4	Double Roles

*Many words have double roles: Each word can be used as a **noun** and as a **verb**, e.g., export, import, respect, seat, book, average.*

Use each word in a sentence, once as a verb and once as a noun.

1. change: a. _____
             b. _____

2. support: a. _____
             b. _____

3. contact: a. _____
             b. _____

4. interest: a. _____
             b. _____

5. force   :   a. _____
             b. _____

Exercise 5	Antonyms

*Some prefixes may be used to make **opposites**, e.g., **un-**, **in-**, **dis-**, **anti-**.*

Give the opposite, i.e., antonym, of each word by using a prefix if possible or by giving a different word.

1. totalitarian   _____   6. freedom   _____

2. fire (a worker) _____   7. frequently   _____

3. continue   _____   8. significant   _____

4. rapid   _____   9. appear   _____

5. rights   _____   10. integrate   _____

Exercise 6	Word Matching

Match words of similar meanings in the two lists.

List A   List B

1. rate   _____   a. connection

2. likely   _____   b. increase

3. sidestep   _____   c. limit

4. extent   _____   d. ignore

5. escalation _____   e. speed

6. contact   _____   f. concession

                                      g. probable

Grammar

Exercise 7	for ... to

Combine the two sentences using for ... to ....

1. The poem is easy. I can learn it by heart.
    The poem is easy for me to learn by heart.
    _____

2.   The chapter is clear. I can understand it.

_____

3.   The pain is slight. I can bear it.

_____

4.   The car is cheap. He can buy it.

_____

5.   The box is light. She can carry it.

_____

6.   The test is easy. I will pass it.

_____

Exercise 8	Prepositions

Add the suitable preposition in each blank.

1.   I have no objection _____ my part.

2.   Prices are increasing _____ a rapid rate.

3.   He   cooperates   _____   them   _____   a   great
     extent.

4.   These factors cannot be ignored _____ the manager.

5.   The supervisor has a close contact _____ the employees.

6.   The situation requires a great deal _____ cooperation _____
     the manager and his employees.

Exercise 9	a, an, the

Add *a*, *an*, or *the* in each blank if necessary.

1.   He shows _____ good attitude towards _____ his colleagues.

2. He is _____ cleverest student in _____ class.

3. It is _____ real challenge to resolve _____ problems when they occur.

4. If _____ employee feels _____ that he is mistreated, he may immediately _____ complain.

5. They have been _____ friends for _____ long period of _____ time.

! " ' : Punctuation ; . ?

Exercise 10	Commas

Add a comma in the square if necessary.

1. If you make ☐ a mistake ☐ you should learn from it.

2. Rain may fall ☐ if it becomes ☐ very cold.

3. While he was writing ☐ she ☐ was cooking.

4. He will finish it ☐ before ☐ you come back.

5. Shakespeare ☐ an English dramatist ☐ was born ☐ in 1564.

6. The book ☐ which I bought last week ☐ is a useful one.

ABCDEFGHI JKLMN Spelling and Dictation OPQRSTUV WXYZ

Exercise 11	ie → y

*Verbs ending in **ie** do not lose **e** if -**ing** is added, an exception to the rule. Instead, **ie** becomes **y**, e.g., die+ing → dying.*

Combine these two units into one word, making any necessary changes.

1. tie + ing   _____   6. challenge + er _____

2. die + ing   _____   7. integrate + ing _____

3. lie + ing   _____   8. manage + ment _____

4. move + ing   _____   9. manage + er   _____

5. hire + ed   _____   10. become + ing _____

Exercise 12	Practice

Practice the spelling of these words.

1. widespread   _____   6. supervisor   _____

2. intelligent   _____   7. accept   _____

3. individual   _____   8. approach   _____

4. consideration _____   9. concession   _____

5. attitude   _____   10. pendulum   _____

Exercise 13	Dictation

You may have any paragraph in the passage or a part of it as a dictation exercise, depending on your instructor's choice.

_____

_____

_____

_____

_____

Pronunciation

Exercise 14	Double Letters

> A **double letter** in English is usually pronounced as a **single letter**, e.g., *passage*.

Pronounce and re-write these words, underlining double letters.

1. challenge _____   6. miss _____

2. controlled _____   7. handicapped _____

3. correct _____   8. stopped _____

4. attitude _____   9. carry _____

5. support _____   10. classroom _____

Exercise 15	Stress

Pronounce and re-write these words, putting the strong stress on the right syllable, e.g., *relátion*.

1. hundred _____   6. occur _____

2. rapid _____   7. attitude _____

3. discrimination _____   8. interest _____

4. consideration _____   9. confrontation _____

5. agitation _____   10. supervisor _____

Free Writing

Exercise 16	Paragraph Writing

Write a ten-line paragraph on the rights of employees. The topic sentence may be this one: *Employees have to get their lawful rights from their employers.*

UNIT 8

THE UNIVERSAL DECLARATION OF HUMAN RIGHTS

(1)

This universal declaration of human rights as a common standard of achievement for all peoples and all nations, to the end that every individual and every organ of society, keeping this Declaration constantly in mind, shall strive by teaching and education to promote respect for these rights and freedoms and by **progressive measures**, national and international, to secure their universal and effective **recognition** and observance, both among the peoples of Member States themselves and among the peoples of territories under their jurisdiction.[1]

Article 1

All human beings are born free and **equal in dignity** and rights. They are endowed with reason and conscience and should act towards one another in a spirit of brotherhood.

Article 2

Everyone is entitled to all

---

[1] The Declaration has thirty articles, but this passage here includes only eleven articles for space reasons.

the **rights** and freedoms set forth in this Declaration, without distinction of any kind, such as race, color, sex, language, religion, political or other opinion, national or social origin, property, birth or other status.

Furthermore, no distinction shall be made on the basis of the political jurisdictional or **international status** of the country or territory to which a person belongs, whether it be independent, trust, non-self-governing, or under any other limitation of **sovereignty**.

(2)

Article 3

Everyone has the right to life, liberty, and **security of person**.

Article 4

No one shall be held in slavery or servitude: slavery and the **slave trade** shall be prohibited in all their forms.

Article 5

No one shall be subjected to **torture** or cruel, inhuman, or degrading treatment or punishment.

Article 6

Everyone has the right to **recognition** everywhere as a person before the law.

Article 7

All are equal before the law and are entitled without any discrimination to **equal**

protection of the law. All are entitled to equal protection against any discrimination in violation of this Declaration and against any incitement to such discrimination.

(3)

Article 8

Everyone has the right to an effective remedy by the competent national tribunals for acts violating the **fundamental rights** granted him by the constitution or by law.

Article 9

No one shall be subjected to **arbitrary arrest**, detention, or exile.

Article 10

Everyone is entitled in full equality to a fair and public hearing by an independent and **impartial tribunal**, in the determination of his rights and obligations and of any criminal charge against him.

Article 11

1. Everyone charged with a **penal offence** has the right to be presumed innocent until proved guilty according to law in a public trial at which he has had all the guarantees necessary for his defense.

2. No one shall be held guilty of any penal offence on account of any act or omission which did not constitute a penal offence, under national or **international law**, at the time when it was committed.

Reading Comprehension

Exercise 1 | **Part 1**

Read Part 1 silently, and then determine whether each statement is true or false according to the text.

1. All humans are free, but not equal.

    _____

2. Brotherhood should prevail among humans.

    _____

3. Humans are endowed with causes and conscience.

    _____

4. Some human races are superior to other races.

    _____

5. These human rights have to be recognized in all countries.

    _____

Exercise 2 | **Part 2**

Read Part 2 silently, and then answer these questions.

1. What is the meaning of "security of person"?

    _____

2. What trade has to be disallowed?

    _____

3. Is torturing prisoners allowed?

    _____

4. How can all be equal before law?

    _____

Listening Comprehension

| Exercise 3 | Part 3 |

Close your book, and listen to your instructor reading   Part 3. Then answer these questions.

1. Is it allowed to exile a person out of his country?

   _____

2. Is everyone guilty until proved innocent?

   _____

3. Should the trial be in public?

   _____

4. Can one be held guilty of an offence that was not so when he committed it?

   _____

5. What does "penal offence" mean?

   _____

Vocabulary

| Exercise 4 | Adjective Derivation |

> *Some suffixes are added to the base to make an adjective such as* **-al, -able,** *-ive, -ent, -ous, -ful, -ic,* *and* **-ical.** *They are called* **adjective-forming suffixes.**

Derive adjectives from these words.

1. education   _____   6. protection   _____

2. reason	_____	7. nation	_____
3. territory	_____	8. constitution	_____
4. security	_____	9. origin	_____
5. independence	_____	10. territory	_____

Exercise 5 | Antonyms

Give the opposite of each word, either by using a prefix or another word.

1. rights	_____	6. dependent	_____
2. national	_____	7. trust	_____
3. effective	_____	8. secure	_____
4. human	_____	9. cruel	_____
5. equality	_____	10. fair	_____

Exercise 6 | Word Matching

Match the words of the two lists looking for similar meanings.

List A		List B
1. discrimination	_____	a. court
2. fundamental	_____	b. crime
3. arbitrary	_____	c. trial
4. hearing	_____	d. distinction
5. tribunal	_____	e. unjustified
6. offence	_____	f. basic
		g. dignity

Grammar

| Exercise 7 | Question-tags |

> The **question-tag** usually consists of two words: an auxiliary and a pronoun. It is preceded by a **comma** and followed by a **question mark**. It is affirmative after a negative statement and negative after an affirmative statement, e.g., He is here, **isn't he**?

Add the suitable question-tag.

1. Everyone is entitled to equality, _____?

2. Everyone charged with an offence has the right to a public trial, _____?

3. Slave trade is totally prohibited, _____?

4. All humans are born free, _____?

5. This Declaration must be observed by all states, _____?

| Exercise 8 | too ... to |

> The structure **too... to** is used to imply negation, e.g., The box is **too** heavy for me **to** carry. It means that I can't carry it.

Combine each pair of sentences using *too*.

1. That question is very difficult. I can't answer it.

    _____

2. This tea is very hot. I can't drink it.

    _____

3. The ceiling is very high. I can't touch it.

    _____

4. The car is very expensive. I can't buy it.

    _____

5. That book is very difficult. I can't understand it.

    _____

Exercise 9	Tenses

Put the bracketed verb in the right form or tense.

1. All humans (to be treated) _____equally.

2. Everyone (bear) _____free.

3. Everyone (have) _____the right to liberty.

4. No one can be (subject) _____to torture.

5. No one may (hold) _____ guilty until proved to be so.

! " " , : Punctuation ; . ?

Exercise 10	Stops and Commas

Add a full stop or comma in the square if necessary.

Yes ☐ my farm is for sale ☐ You can have it ☐ at a very low price ☐

I'm going to the city ☐ to get a job in a factory ☐ and work only ☐ five days

a week ☐ I don't have enough time for it ☐

ABCDEFGHI JKLMN   Spelling and Dictation   OPQRSTUV WXYZ

Exercise 11 | Omission of the Final e

If a suffix beginning with a vowel is added to a word ending in silent e, this e is usually omitted, e.g., take + ing → taking.

Re-write these combinations, omitting the final e where necessary.

1. write + ing = _____

2. write + er = _____

3. receive + ing = _____

4. move + ment = _____

5. cause + al = _____

6. name + ing = _____

7. bite + ing = _____

8. large + ness = _____

9. huge + ness = _____

10. note + ing = _____

Exercise 12 | Practice

Practice the spelling of these words.

1. entitle _____

2. constitution _____

3. tribunal _____

4. guarantee _____

5. offence _____

6. protection _____

7. recognition _____

8. punishment _____

9. arbitrary _____

10. exile _____

Exercise 13 | Dictation

You may have any paragraph in the passage or a part of it as a dictation exercise, depending on your instructor's choice.

_____

_____

_____

_____

_____

Pronunciation

| Exercise 14 | Stress |

Pronounce and re-write these words, putting the strong stress on the right syllable, e.g., window.

1. conscience _____   6. another _____

2. language _____   7. reason _____

3. country _____   8. themselves _____

4. limitation _____   9. under _____

5. liberty _____   10. individual _____

| Exercise 15 | Stress |

Pronounce and re-write these words putting the strong stress on the right syllable, e.g., táble.

1. standard _____   6. dignity _____

2. territories _____   7. observance _____

3. language _____   8. themselves _____

4. property _____   9. declaration _____

5. national _____   10. discrimination _____

Free Writing

| Exercise 16 | Paragraph Writing |

Write a ten-line paragraph on the Declaration of Human Rights. Here is the topic sentence, i.e., the first sentence in the paragraph: *The Declaration of Human Rights emphasizes several principles.*

_____

_____

_____

_____

_____

_____

_____

_____

_____

_____

Unit 9

INDUSTRIES FROM FORESTS

(1)

Forests all over the world consist of trees. They have grown naturally without the help of man, but where the trees have been cut down it is often necessary to plant young ones to take their place. So, in some parts of the world there are now huge **plantations** made by man. The chief product of all forests is 5   wood or **timber**. If the trees are large, the timber is called "**lumber**" and is used for house building and all work where large baulks of timber are required. In Britain and many parts of the world, smaller trees are cut down for poles, fencing posts, pit-props, etc.**Wood pulp** (for paper) is made usually from trees

10 scarcely large enough for lumber. Then there are many "**minor forest products**". Some forests are most valued as a source of firewood; many trees yield gums and oils or are valued for their bark.

(2)

Some wood is much softer and easier to saw than others. The "**soft wood**", of which ordinary boxes and packing cases are made, is quite different from the

15 "**hard woods**" used for chairs and other furniture. So there are two main types of timber.

Softwoods, used generally for building as well as for pit-props, making wood-pulp, boxes, and cheaper furniture, such as kitchen tables, are obtained mainly from the **coniferous** (cone-

20 bearing) trees of the cold temperate and northern forests.

Hardwoods, used for furniture, ornamental wood-work, the fittings, and decks of ships, are mainly

25 obtained from broad-leafed trees-both the **deciduous trees** of temperate and tropical forests and the **evergreen trees** of equatorial forests.

Of all the wood used in the

30 world, only about 2 per cent is hardwood from **tropical forests,** 18 per cent hardwood from temperate forests, whilst the rest, 80 per cent, is softwood from the great coniferous

35 forests.

(3)

In the **equatorial forests,** the giant trees are usually of hardwood. Often the timber is very beautiful and in many cases is easy to work with and makes
40   beautiful furniture and paneling (such as we now often see in railway carriages). There are several reasons why these forests are still little **exploited**. The chief reason is that there are hundreds of different trees in the forests, and it is difficult to pick out and then to cut down the five or six kinds which may be needed. If all the trees are cut down, it is difficult to sell all the many different
45   kinds of timber. So, small quantities of beautiful timber, such as mahogany and rosewood, come from the hot wet forests of South and Central America and West Africa. Some of the **equatorial trees** yield rubber, and the chief rubber tree is a native of South America. Most of the world's **rubber** is now obtained from plantations. In West Africa the oil palm grows wild, but much of the oil is now
50   obtained from palms which have been planted. From the forests of Malaya come the rattan and Malacca canes often used in the making of walking-sticks.

Reading Comprehension

Exercise 1 | **Part 1**

Read Part 1 silently, and then answer these questions.

1. What does a forest consist of?

2. Are all forests natural ones?

3. What is the main product of forests?

4. What is the difference between timber and lumber?

5. Are fencing posts made from large trees or smaller ones?

Exercise 2 | **Part 2**

Read Part 2 silently, and then answer these questions.

1. What are the two types of wood?

2. Are boxes made from softwood or hardwood?

3. What kind of wood is given by equatorial forests?

4. What wood is given by coniferous forests?

5. What wood is used more in the world?

Listening Comprehension

Exercise 3 | Part 3

Close your book, and listen to your instructor reading   Part 3. Then determine whether each statement is true or false according to the text.

1. Giant trees give softwood.   _____

2. Some trees in South America give rubber.   _____

3. Most rubber in the world comes from natural forests.   _____

4. Walking-sticks come from the forests of West Africa.   _____

Vocabulary

Exercise 4 | Word Selection

Fill in each blank with a suitable word: lumber, coniferous, temperate, deciduous, evergreen, tropical, equatorial.

1. Forests around the equator are called _____ forests.

2. Trees that drop their leaves every autumn _____ trees.

3. Trees that bear cones are called _____ trees.

4. Trees that keep their leaves are called _____ trees.

5. The wood of large trees is called _____ .

Exercise 5 | Antonyms

Give the opposite of each word, not by prefixing.

1. natural	_____	6. cheap	_____
2. necessary	_____	7. different	_____
3. major	_____	8. easy	_____
4. deciduous	_____	9. wet	_____
5. soft	_____	10. hot	_____

Exercise 6	**Verb Derivation**

> Some affixes are used to make verbs, e.g., **-ize**, **en-**, **-en**, and **-ify**. They are called **verb-forming affixes**.

Derive verbs from these words; the answer is sometimes the same word without any change.

1. natural	_____	6. soft	_____
2. help	_____	7. hard	_____
3. product	_____	8. forest	_____
4. large	_____	9. different	_____
5. value	_____	10. ornamental	_____

Grammar

Exercise 7	**Wh-words**

> Wh-words include **who**, **whom**, **whose**, **what**, **which**, **why**, **when**, **where**, and **how**. They are called as such because most of them begin with **wh-**.

Add a suitable wh-word in each blank.

1. He does not know _____ to go in France.

2. He has not decided _____ to leave, but it will be soon.

3. Little by little they will learn _____ to do things better.

4. He does not know the answer, but he will find _____ to ask, probably one of his teachers.

5. He's in real trouble, and he doesn't know _____ to do.

Exercise 8	The Passive Voice

> The passive must contain a verb **to be** and **Form 3**, i.e., the past participle, e.g., *was written. It may contain other auxiliaries as well, e.g., will be written.*

Change these sentences to passive.

1. They call it wood or timber.

    _____

2. Farmers cut some trees for firewood.

    _____

3. They have made boxes from softwood.

    _____

4. They will obtain hardwood from broad-leafed trees.

    _____

5. Some trees yield rubber.

    _____

Exercise 9	The Active Voice

Change these sentences from passive to active.

1. The results will be announced next week.

    _____

2.   The books have been distributed by the bookshop.

_____

3.   The answer sheets are being graded by the teacher.

_____

4.   Rubber is obtained from plantations by farmers.

_____

5.   He was visited several times by his uncle.

_____

| Exercise 10 | The Apostrophe |

*The apostrophe is used with the **possessive**, e.g., Ali's book. It is also used with **contractions**, e.g., he'll. It is used in **unusual plurals** as well, e.g., 4's, m's.*

Add capital letters, stops, and apostrophes where necessary.

1.   hes fond of swimming it is a very good sport

_____

2.   ill give a summary of the reasons for the second world war

_____

3.   theyre looking for their bags and johns books

_____

4.   dont worry about it

_____

5.   these are the doctors cars

_____

ABCDEFGHI JKLMN	**Spelling and Dictation**	OPQRSTUV WXYZ

Exercise 11	Doubling the Final Consonant

If you add a suffix beginning with a vowel to a word ending in a consonant preceded by a short stressed vowel, the consonant is doubled, e.g., drop + ing → dropping, with some exceptions.

Combine these two units into one word making any necessary changes.

1. run + er   _____   6. cut + ing   _____

2. swim + ing   _____   7. spend + ing   _____

3. speak + er   _____   8. sell + er   _____

4. answer + ing   _____   9. win + er   _____

5. stand + ing   _____   10. dig + ing   _____

Exercise 12	Practice

Practice the spelling of these words.

1. plantations   _____   6. temperate   _____

2. fencing   _____   7. mahogany   _____

3. furniture   _____   8. equatorial   _____

4. coniferous   _____   9. beautiful   _____

5. deciduous   _____   10. product   _____

Exercise 13	Dictation

You may have any paragraph in the passage or a part of it as a dictation exercise, depending on your instructor's choice.

_____

_____

_____

_____

Pronunciation

Exercise 14 | **Silent *l***

> If the letter *l* comes after a vowel and before a consonant, it **may** be silent, e. g., talk.

Pronounce and re-write these words, putting a dot under the silent letter.

1. talk _____   5. could _____
2. chalk _____   6. half _____
3. walk _____   7. calf _____
4. would _____   8. should _____

Exercise 15 | **Stress**

Pronounce and re-write these words, putting the strong stress on the right syllable, e.g., náture.

1. nature _____   6. generally _____
2. fencing _____   7. timber _____
3. firewood _____   8. product _____

4. different   _____   9. packing   _____

5. cheaper   _____   10. plantation   _____

Free Writing

Exercise 16	Paragraph Writing

Write a ten-line paragraph on the different usages of wood. The topic sentence may run like this: Wood is used in different ways in our life.

_____

_____

_____

_____

_____

_____

_____

_____

_____

_____

Unit 10

PUBLIC AND PRIVATE SECTORS

(1)

The expressions "public sector" and "private sector" are now very commonplace. The first refers to a system of organizations concerned with achieving State purposes. **Public sector** organizations include Government Departments, local authorities, and nationalized industries. There is tremendous
5 variety within this sector. The term "**private sector**", on the other hand, is used

as a collective phrase referring to organizations which are neither State-owned nor operating specifically to achieve State goals.

(2)

A popular view of the **private organization** is that it is built on the
10　enterprise　　　of　　　an　　　individual　　　or　　　a　　　family,　　　the typical example of such an organization being the business firm. Another linked view of such organizations is that they are headed by an entrepreneur, and ownership and control of the business are in his hands. Such a
15　view of the business firm is much loved by **classical economists**, and whole industries are sometimes portrayed as being organized in this way. Competition takes place
20　between the firms, and as a result everybody benefits. Efficiency is rewarded and inefficiency is punished. Such a view of **private business** organization is no longer
25　appropriate; the day of the

individual entrepreneur, with notable exceptions, is over. However, this model is a useful means of illustrating the widely reported differences between the public and the private sectors.

(3)

The first test of this difference is known as the **beneficiary test**. This test
30　asks this question: who benefits from the organization? Or, put another way, whose goals does the organization serve? The **main beneficiary** of the firm which is headed by a single individual and financedby his money is the

owner/manager. The owner usually invests time and effort in establishing a
35 business in the hope of making a profit. Profit is seen as the main motivating
force of a private enterprise economy. The administration of such a firm is
concerned with the **management** of men, materials, and the like, in such a way
as to make it possible and practical to make a profit. Administration here is also
concerned with the problem of "**efficiency**".

40 When the beneficiary test is applied to the State organizations of the public
sector, different results are obtained. For instance, it is difficult to recognize who
the prime beneficiaries of many **public sector organizations** are. Is the **prime
beneficiary** of the Department of Social Security the Minister in charge of it? Is it
an individual applicant for welfare benefit at the counter of a **local branch** of the
45 Department?

📖 Reading Comprehension 📖

Exercise 1	Part 1

Read Part 1 silently, and then determine whether these statements are true or false according to the text.

1. The term "public sector" is a rarely used term.

---

2. "Public sector" refers to government institutions.

---

3. The term "private sector" is part of the term "public sector".

---

4. Nationalized industries are owned by the private sector.

Exercise 2	Part 2

Read Part 2 silently, and then answer these questions.

1. What is the popular view of the private organization?

---

2. Is the business firm a model of the public sector?

---

3. Who is the usual head of a private-sector organization?

---

4. Is this popular view still accepted nowadays?

Listening Comprehension

Exercise 3	Part 3

Close your book, and listen to your instructor reading   Part 3. Then answer these questions.

1. What test is used to find out whether the organization belongs to the private or public sector?

    _____

2. Who is the main beneficiary of an individual-owned firm?

    _____

3. What is the meaning of "the owner/manager"?

    _____

4. What is the main purpose of the private sector?

    _____

Vocabulary

Exercise 4	Adjective Derivation

Derive adjectives from these words.

1. sector   _____   6. differ   _____

2. organization   _____   7. finance   _____

3. department   _____   8. practice   _____

4. collect   _____   9. problem   _____

5. efficiency   _____   10. industry   _____

| Exercise 5 | Meanings of Suffixes |

What is the meaning of the underlined suffix in these words? Give two more examples of each suffix.

1. organiza<u>tion</u>   _____   _____   _____

2. popul<u>ar</u>   _____   _____   _____

3. busi<u>ness</u>   _____   _____   _____

4. secur<u>ity</u>   _____   _____   _____

5. applic<u>ant</u>   _____   _____   _____

| Exercise 6 | Word Matching |

Match the words of similar meanings in the two lists.

List A		List B
1. organization	_____	a. objective
2. purpose	_____	b. based
3. specifically	_____	c. suitable
4. built	_____	d. especially
5. linked	_____	e. management
6. appropriate	_____	f. related
		g. institution

Grammar

| Exercise 7 | Wh- questions |

***Who** and **whom** are used to ask about persons, **what** about things, **where** about places, **when** about times, **why** about reasons, and **how** about manners.*

Ask about the underlined unit using a suitable wh-word.

1. <u>Different results</u> are obtained.

    _____

2. <u>The owner</u> invests his time in order to make a profit.

    _____

3. He does his assignments <u>immediately after lunch</u>.

    _____

4. She missed the bus <u>because she got up late</u>.

    _____

5. He will establish a business <u>in Sidney in Australia</u>.

    _____

Exercise 8	Conditional Sentences

> In addition to the three well-known types of conditional sentences, there are many other types. One of them is that used in **science**, where the two verbs are **present simple**, e.g., *If you <u>heat</u> ice, it <u>melts</u>.*

Put the verbs in brackets in their suitable tenses.

1. If water (become) _____ colder and colder, it (freeze) _____.

2. If a substance (heat) _____ it (expand) _____.

3. If you study, you (pass) _____.

4. If you had studied, you (pass) _____.

5. I shall answer him if he (ask) _____ me.

6. Had I seen him, I (tell) _____ him.

7. If a piece of wood is thrown on water, it (float) _____.

8. He would have come if you (invite) _____ him.

9. If you see him, (tell) _____ him about the time of the test.

10. If I saw him, I (tell) _____ him.

Exercise 9	A Special Pattern

> *You may have a number plus a hyphen plus a singular countable noun as a* **premodifier** *of a noun, e.g., a two-hour test.*

Change these sentences using such a pattern: *It is a three-floor building.*

1. This train has forty carriages.

_____

2. This bus can take sixty passengers.

_____

3. The trip to Paris takes five days.

_____

4. The lorry can carry two tons.

_____

5. The examination will last two hours.

_____

6. The book has 300 pages.

_____

7. This building has five floors.

_____

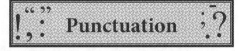

Exercise 10	Review

Add capital letters and punctuation marks where necessary. It is better to re-write the paragraph in the space given.

now you know your friends my son they did not give you a bed they did not invite you to dinner they did not lend you even a little money in fact not one of them offered you any help at all do you call these real friends i your father am your real friend you must learn the difference between a whole-friend a half-friend and a no-friend

_____

_____

_____

_____

_____

ABCDEFGHI JKLMN	**Spelling and Dictation**	OPQRSTUV WXYZ

Exercise 11	c → ck

> *If the final consonant is c preceded by a short vowel and a suffix beginning with a vowel is added, c will become ck, e.g., picnic+ ed→ picnicked.*

Combine these units into one word, making any necessary changes.

1. picnic + ed _____   **6.** hot + est _____

2. traffic + ing _____   **7.** plan + ing _____

3. picnic + ing _____   **8.** proceed + ing _____

4. traffic + ed _____   **9.** forget + ing _____

5. red + er _____   **10.** begin + ing _____

Exercise 12	Practice

Practice the spelling of these words.

1. public   _____   6. problem   _____

2. authority   _____   7. administration   _____

3. inefficiency   _____   8. beneficiary   _____

4. business   _____   9. recognize   _____

5. operating   _____   10. illustrate   _____

Exercise 13	Dictation

You may have any paragraph in the passage or a part of it as a dictation exercise, depending on your instructor's choice.

_____

_____

_____

_____

_____

Pronunciation

Exercise 14	The Final e

*The final **e** is usually **silent**; there are a few exceptions, however, e.g., payee.*

Pronounce and re-write these words, putting dots under silent letters.

1. translate	_____	7. manage	_____
2. purpose	_____	8. instance	_____
3. achieve	_____	9. attaché	_____
4. use	_____	10. fiancé	_____
5. organize	_____	11. trainee	_____
6. difference	_____	12. employee	_____

Exercise 15	Stress

Pronounce and re-write these words, putting the strong stress on the right syllable, e.g., búsiness.

1. problem	_____	6. motivate	_____
2. materials	_____	7. economy	_____
3. practical	_____	8. profit	_____
4. concerned	_____	9. invest	_____
5. obtain	_____	10. effort	_____

✍ Free Writing ✍

Exercise 16	Paragraph Writing

Write a ten-line paragraph about the differences between the private sector and the public sector.

_____

_____

Unit 11

Mr. PHILEAS FOGG

(1)

Mr. Phileas Fogg lived, in 1872, at No. 7, Saville Row, Burlington Gardens, the house in which Sheridan died in 1814. He was one of the most **prominent members** of the London Reform Club, though he never did anything to attract attention; a strange character about whom little was known except that he was a **polished man** of the world. People said that he resembled Byron-at least that his head was Byronic; but he was a **bearded**, tranquil Byron, who might live on a thousand years without growing old.

An Englishman, indeed it was more doubtful whether Phileas Fogg was a Londoner. He was never seen on Change, nor at the

10 Bank, nor in the counting rooms of the "City"; no ships of which he was the owner ever came into **London docks**; he had no **public employment**; he had never been entered at any of the Inns of Court, either at the Temple, or Lincoln's Inn, or Gray's Inn; nor had his voice ever resounded in the Court of Chancery, or in the Exchequer, or the Queen's Bench, or the Ecclesiastical Courts. He
15 certainly was not **a manufacturer**; nor was he a merchant or a gentleman farmer. His name was unfamiliar to the scientific and **learned societies**, and he never was known to take part in the deliberations of the **Royal Institution** or the London Institution, the Artisan's Association or the Institution of Arts and Sciences. He belonged, in fact, to none of the numerous societies which swarm in the English
20 capital, from the Harmonica Society to that of the **Entomologists**, founded mainly for the purpose of abolishing pernicious insects. Phileas Fogg was a member of the Reform, and that was all.

(2)

The way in which he got **admission** to this exclusive club was
25 simple enough. He was recommended by the Barings Brothers, with whom he had an open credit. His checks were regularly paid on sight from his account, which was always flush.

30 Was Phileas Fogg rich? Undoubtedly. But those who know him best could not imagine how he had made his fortune, and Mr. Fogg was the last person to whom
35 to apply for the **information**. He was not lavish, nor, on the contrary, stingy; for whenever he knew that

money was needed for a noble, useful, or **benevolent purpose**, he supplied
40 it quietly, and sometimes anonymously. He was, in short, the least
communicative of men. He talked very little, and seemed all the more
mysterious for his taciturn manner. His daily habits were quite open to
observation; but whatever he did was so precisely what he had always done
before, that the wits of the curious were fairly puzzled.

(3)

45   Had he traveled? It was likely, for no one seemed to be so familiar with
the world; there was no spot so secluded that he did not have an **intimate
acquaintance** with. He often corrected, with a few clear words, the
thousand conjectures advanced by **members of the club** as to lost and
unheard-of travelers; he would point out the true probabilities, seem as if
50 gifted with a sort of second sight, so often did events justify his **predictions**.
He must have traveled everywhere, at least in the spirit.

In any case, it was certain that Phileas Fogg had not absented himself
from London for many years. Those who had the honor of a closer
acquaintance with him than the
55 rest declared that nobody could
claim to have ever seen him
anywhere else. His sole **pastimes**
were reading the papers and
playing whist. He often won at
60 this game, which, as a silent one,

harmonized with his nature; his winnings never went into his purse, but
were **reserved** as a fund for his charities.

Reading Comprehension

| Exercise 1 | Part 1 |

Read Part 1 silently, and then determine whether these statements are true or false according to the text.

1. Mr. Fogg was a member of the London Reform Club.

    _____

2. Mr. Fogg was a government employee.

    _____

3. Mr. Fogg had a very large farm.

    _____

4. Mr. Fogg was not a trader.

    _____

5. Mr. Fogg was a famous man of industry.

    _____

| Exercise 2 | Part 2 |

Read Part 2 silently, and then answer these questions.

1. How was Mr. Fogg admitted to the club?

    _____

2. Was he a rich man?

    _____

3. Was he a spendthrift or a miser?

    _____

4. Did he like to talk to people?

    _____

5. Did people know his daily habits?

_____

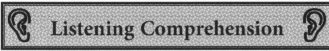

Listening Comprehension

| Exercise 3 | Part 3 |

Close your book, and listen to your instructor reading   Part 3. Then answer these questions.

1. Did Mr. Fogg know the world around him?

_____

2. How did he pass his time?

_____

3. What did he do with his winnings?

_____

4. Was he a charitable person?

_____

Vocabulary

| Exercise 4 | Verb Derivation |

Derive verbs from these words.

1. information   _____   5. habit   _____

2. puzzle   _____   6. observation   _____

3. imagination   _____   7. exclusive   _____

4. familiar _____   8. manufacturer _____

Exercise 5	Word Production

Give one word for each phrase; the first two letters of the answer are given.

1. to improve matters: re _____

2. a person living in London: Lo _____

3. a person living in New York: Ne _____

4. a man of industry: ma _____

5. a man working at a farm: fa _____

6. between lavish and stingy: mo _____

7. ready to do good to people: be _____

Exercise 6	Matching Words

Match the words of similar meanings in the two lists.

List A		List B
1. character	_____	a. state
2. polished	_____	b. kill
3. public	_____	c. surely
4. take part	_____	d. educated
5. abolish	_____	e. participate
6. undoubtedly	_____	f. mysteriously
		g. personality

Grammar

Exercise 7 | Reported Imperative

> To change **direct imperatives** into reported or indirect speech, we use a **reporting verb** plus **to**, e.g., Get ready ⟹ He **told** them **to** get ready.

Change these direct imperatives into reported speech.

1. Do your homework without delay.

_____

2. Get ready for the test tomorrow.

_____

3. Don't postpone today's work until tomorrow.

_____

4. Be neither a lender nor a borrower.

_____

5. Study day by day, not month by month.

_____

Exercise 8 | Reported Questions

> To change **direct wh-questions** into reported ones, you need a reporting verb, e.g., asked, wanted to know. Then you have to cancel any **subject-verb inversion**. Verb tenses have to be changed if the reporting verb is past, and the question mark is replaced by a stop, e.g., Where are they? ⟹ He wanted to know where they were.

Change these direct wh-questions into indirect speech.

1. Why did he come so late?

   He wanted to know _____

2. Where is my book?

   _____

3. What has happened?

   _____

4. When will he arrive?

   _____

5. Who did it?

   _____

Exercise 9	Reported Statements

> To report statements, you need a suitable **reporting verb** like **said**. You use the conjunction **that** as well. Tenses and pronouns also require some modification, e.g., *They will come* $\implies$ *He said that they would come.*

Change these direct statements into indirect speech.

1. He was not a manufacturer.

   He said that _____

2. He will visit us tomorrow.

   _____

3. I am doing my homework now.

   _____

4. They have done the job very well.

   _____

5. She was never seen at the bank.

   _____

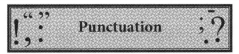

Punctuation

| Exercise 10 | Mark Addition |

Add capital letters and punctuation marks wherever necessary.

1. who has taken away the book which had pictures of london

2. my uncle jack who lives in stratford has a car which he keeps in mr browns garage and another which he keeps in london

3. huda you havent posted salmas letter youd better hurry and post it at once

4. the educational system which you can read about in the last two magazines is one of the most advanced in the region

ABCDEFGHI JKLMN	Spelling and Dictation	OPQRSTUV WXYZ

Exercise 11 — Contractions

> *Contractions require two things. First, put an **apostrophe** in the place of the omitted letter or letters. Second, combine the two words into one word, e.g., has not* ⟹ *hasn't.*

Make contractions using the apostrophe, e.g., must not → mustn't.

1. had + not _____   6. I + shall _____

2. can + not _____   7. they + have _____

3. shall + not _____   8. she + is _____

4. will + not _____   9. are + not _____

5. he + had _____   10. has + not _____

Exercise 12 — Practice

Practice the spelling of these words.

1. resemble _____   6. correct _____

2. unfamiliar _____   7. acquaintance _____

3. association _____   8. pastime _____

4. institution _____   9. harmonize _____

5. observation _____   10. motionless _____

Exercise 13   Dictation

You may have any paragraph in the passage or a part of it as a dictation exercise, depending on your instructor's choice.

_____
_____
_____
_____

■ Pronunciation ■

Exercise 14	Initial kn

> If **k** is initial before **n**, it becomes silent, e.g., **knife**.

Pronounce and re-write these words, putting a dot under any silent letter.

1. knight   _____   7. knock   _____

2. know   _____   8. knowledge   _____

3. knit   _____   9. knitting   _____

4. knee   _____   10. knives   _____

5. kneel   _____   11. kill   _____

6. knob   _____   12. kite   _____

Exercise 15	Stress

Pronounce and re-write these words, putting the strong stress on the right syllable, e.g., indeéd.

1. public   _____   6. imagine   _____

2. association _____   7. manner _____

3. reform _____   8. nobody _____

4. indeed _____   9. motionless _____

5. benevolent _____   10. precisely _____

✍ Free Writing ✍

Exercise 16	Paragraph Writing

Write a ten-line paragraph about the character of a person whom you know very well such as your father, brother, or friend.

_____

_____

_____

_____

_____

_____

_____

_____

_____

Unit 12

WHAT IS LINGUISTICS?

(1)

The field of linguistics, the scientific study of the human natural language, is a growing and interesting area of study, with an important effect on fields as diverse as education, anthropology, sociology, language teaching, cognitive psychology, philosophy, **computer science**, neuroscience, and **artificial**
5   **intelligence**, among others. Indeed the last five fields cited, along with linguistics, are the key components of the emerging field of **cognitive science**, the study of the structure and functioning of human cognitive processes.

In spite of the importance of the field of linguistics, many people, even highly **educated people**, will tell you that they have only a vague idea of
10   what the field is about. Some believe that a

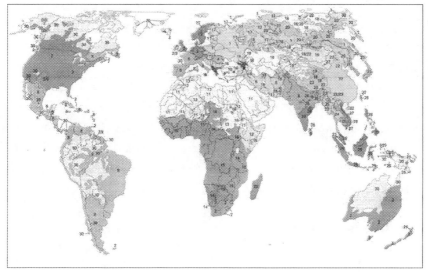

linguist is a person who speaks several languages fluently. Others believe that linguists are **language experts** who can help you decide whether it is better to say "It is I" or "It's me". Yet it is quite possible to be a
15   **professional linguist** (and an excellent one at that) without having taught a single language class, without having interpreted at the UN, and without speaking any more than one language.

(2)

What is linguistics then? Fundamentally, the field is concerned with the nature of language and communication. It is apparent that people have
20   been fascinated with language and **communication** for thousands of years, yet in many ways we are only beginning to understand the **complex nature** of this aspect of human life. If we ask about the nature of language or how communication works, we quickly realize that these questions have no simple answers and are much too broad to be answered in a direct way.
25   Similarly, questions such as "What is energy?" or "What is matter?" cannot be answered in a **simple fashion**, and indeed the entire field of physics is an attempt to answer them.

Linguistics is no different: the field as a whole represents an attempt to break down the **broad questions** about the nature of language and
30   communication into smaller, more **manageable questions** that we can hope to answer, and in so doing establish reasonable results that we can build on in moving closer to answers to the larger questions. Unless we limit our sights in this way and **restrict** ourselves to particular frameworks for examining different aspects of language and **communication**, we cannot
35   hope to make progress in answering the broad questions that have fascinated people for so long. As we will see, the field covers a surprisingly broad range of **topics** related to language and communication.

(3)

40   Chapter 1 of the book deals primarily with the structural components of language. Chapter 2, "*Morphology*", is concerned with the properties of words and **word-building** rules.   Chapter 3, "*Phonetics* and *Phonemic Transcription*", introduces the **physiology** involved in the production of speech sounds as well as phonemic and phonetic **transcription systems** that are used to represent the

45 sounds of English. Chapter 4, "*Phonology*", surveys the **organizational principles** that determine the patterns the speech sounds are subject to. Chapter 5, "*Syntax*", presents a study of the structure of sentences and

50 phrases. Chapter 6, "*Semantics*", surveys the **properties** of meaning and denotation. Chapter 7, "*Language Variation*", deals with the ways speakers and groups of speakers can differ from each other in terms of the

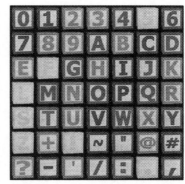

55 various forms of language that they use. Chapter 8, "*Language Change*", examines how languages change over time and how language can be historically related.

Reading Comprehension

Exercise 1 | **Part 1**

    Read Part 1 silently, and then determine whether these statements are true or false according to the text.

1.   Does linguistics affect education?

2.   What fields are affected by linguistics as well?

_____

3.   Should a linguist know at least two languages?

_____

4.   Should a linguist be a teacher of language?

_____

| Exercise 2 | Part 2 |

Read Part 2 silently, and then determine whether these statements are true or false.

1.   Linguistics studies the nature of language.

_____

2.   Linguistics also studies the nature of communication.

_____

3.   Questions about the nature of language are easy to answer.

_____

4.   Questions about the nature of energy and matter are easy to answer as well.

_____

Listening Comprehension

| Exercise 3 | Part 3 |

Close your book, and listen to your instructor reading   Part 3. Then determine whether each statement is true or false.

1.   Phonology studies the production of speech sounds.

_____

2. Syntax deals with sentence structure.

   _____

3. Semantics deals with word building.

   _____

4. Morphology deals with the patterns of speech sounds.

   _____

Vocabulary

Exercise 4 — Meanings of Affixes

*Remember that every **prefix** or **suffix** has a meaning, e.g., re- in "re-write" means "again".*

What are the meanings of these underlined units?

1. linguistics   _____   6. organizational _____

2. computer   _____   7. represent   _____

3. components   _____   8. progress   _____

4. linguist   _____   9. reasonable   _____

5. communication _____   10. realize   _____

Exercise 5 — Noun Derivation

One way to make nouns is to add -er to the verb, e.g., learner, swimmer, runner. This suffix is a noun-forming suffix, and it means "doer" or "agent".

Derive nouns from these words.

1. speak   _____   8. excellent   _____

2. preach	_____	9. complex	_____
3. dive	_____	10. simple	_____
4. hear	_____	11. manageable	_____
5. teach	_____	12. close	_____
6. believe	_____	13. restrict	_____
7. apparent	_____	14. attempt	_____

Exercise 6	Word Matching

Match words of similar meanings in the two lists.

List A		List B
1. importance	_____	**a.** specialist
2. expert	_____	**b.** complete
3. apparent	_____	**c.** denotation
4. realize	_____	**d.** know
5. entire	_____	**e.** emerge
		f. clear
		g. significance

Grammar

Exercise 7	Active ⟹ Passive

Passivization partly requires fronting the object and placing the subject at the end of the sentence preceded by "by". This "**by-structure**" is usually optional, e.g., The boy ate the apple ⟹ The apple was eaten (by the boy).

Change these active sentences to the passive voice.

1. They have built a solid system.

   _____

2. They have studied different fields of the science.

   _____

3. The research has analyzed some samples of the language.

   _____

4. He will have finished filing by 5 o'clock.

   _____

5. She will have done it by tomorrow.

   _____

Exercise 8	A Special Pattern

The pattern [**Infinitive+Be+Subject Complement**] *can be transformed into this pattern: It+Be+Subject Complement+ Infinitive, e.g., To read is useful* ⟹ *It is useful to read.*

Change these sentences, using It ... to *instead of to.*

1. To give is better than to take.

   _____

2. To smoke is harmful.

   _____

3. To study day by day is better.

   _____

4. To tell the truth is better than to remain silent.

   _____

5. To eat a little is better than to overeat.

   _____

Exercise 9	Relative Pronouns

> The relative "**that**" can often replace **who**, **whom**, or **which** in adjective clauses. It can also refer to humans and non-humans.

Combine these pairs of sentences using wh-words **or** that.

1. This is my *friend. He* came from Paris yesterday.

    _____

2. I like to read the *book.* You read *it* last week.

    _____

3. He is a good *friend.* You can depend on *him.*

    _____

4. This is the *boy. His* bicycle was lost.

    _____

5. He was looking for the *wallet.* He found *it* later.

    _____

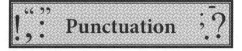

Exercise 10	Mark Addition

> In **direct speech**, a comma is put before the speech, inverted commas are opened before the speech and closed after, a capital letter appears at the beginning, and a stop, question mark, or exclamation mark at the end, e.g., He said, "They have arrived".

Add capital letters and the suitable punctuation marks to these direct-speech sentences, wherever necessary.

1.   he asked can you speak chinese

_____

2.   she answered no

_____

3.   he asked what languages can you speak

_____

4.   she said greek and Turkish

_____

5.   he asked what else

_____

6.   she replied only those two

_____

ABCDEFGHI JKLMN   Spelling and Dictation   OPQRSTUV WXYZ

Exercise 11 | full → ful

> When **full** is combined with a previous word, it becomes **ful**, e.g., handful.

Combine these two units into one word, making any necessary changes in spelling.

1. beauty + full   _____   5. spoon + full   _____

2. care + full   _____   6. wonder + full   _____

3. thank + full   _____   7. mouth + full   _____

4. grate + full   _____   8. health + full   _____

Exercise 12	Practice

Practice the spelling of these words.

1. psychology   _____   6. communication _____

2. function   _____   7. whether   _____

3. linguistics   _____   8. emerge   _____

4. fascinated   _____   9. expert   _____

5. fundamental   _____   10. manageable   _____

Exercise 13	Dictation

You may have any paragraph in the passage or a part of it as a dictation exercise, depending on your instructor's choice.

_____

_____

_____

_____

_____

■ Pronunciation ■

Exercise 14	the

*When **the** is stressed, it is /ðiy/. When before a consonant, it is /ðə/, e.g., the book. When before a vowel, it is /ði/, e.g., the apple.*

Pronounce these phrases, and fill in the blanks with the correct pronunciation of the article the, i.e., /ðiy/, /ðə/, or /ði/.

1. the school   _____   6. thé homework   _____

2. the university   _____   7. the hotel   _____

3. the umbrella   _____   8. the attempt_____

4. thé garden   _____   9. the answer   _____

5. the house   _____   10. thé test   _____

Exercise 15	Stress

Pronounce and re-write these words, putting the strong stress on the right syllable, e.g., befóre.

1. cognitive   _____   6. about   _____

2. component   _____   7. answered   _____

3. without   _____   8. progress   _____

4. believe   _____   9. establish   _____

5. educated   _____   10. fashion   _____

✍ Free Writing ✍

Exercise 16	Paragraph Writing

Write a ten-line paragraph about the nature of language or the importance of language.

_____

_____

Unit 13

ADVERTISING AND
MARKETING

(1)

Marketing is more than just distributing goods from the manufacturer
to the **final customer**. It includes all the stages between creation of the
product and the after-market which follows the **final sale**. One of these
stages is advertising. The stages are like links in a chain, and the chain will
5   break if one of the links is weak. **Advertising** is, therefore, as important as
every other stage or link, and each depends on the other for success.

The product or service itself, its naming, packaging, pricing, and **distribution** are all reflected in advertising, which has been called the
10 lifeblood of an organization. Without advertising, the products or services cannot flow to the distributors or sellers and on to the **consumers** or users.

(2)

Advertising belongs to the modern **industrial world** and to those countries which are developing and becoming industrialized. In the past when a shopkeeper or stall holder had only to show and shout his goods to
15 passers-by, advertising as we know it today hardly existed. Early forms of advertising were signs such as the inn sign, the red-and-white striped barber's pole, the apothecary's jars of colored liquid, and the
20 wheelwright's wheel, some of which have survived until today.

The need for advertising developed with the expansion of population and the growth of towns with their shops and large stores, **mass**
25 **production** in factories, roads, and railways to convey goods and popular newspapers in which to advertise. The large quantities of goods being produced were made known by means of advertising to unknown customers who lived far from the **place of manufacture**.

(3)

If one looks at old pictures of horse buses in, say, late nineteenth-century
30 London, one will see that they carry **advertisements** for products famous today, a proof of the effectiveness of advertising. Thus, the modern world depends on

advertising. Without it, **producers** and **distributors** would be unable to sell, buyers would not know about and continue to remember **products** or
35 services, and the modern industrial world would collapse. If factory output is to be maintained profitably, advertising must be powerful and continuous. Mass production requires mass consumption, which in turn requires advertising to the mass market through the **mass media**.

In the "North" (i.e., the **industrialized countries** of the world) it is easy
40 to take this process **for granted**. So used are people to buying **well-known goods** that they often criticize advertising. They sometimes complain that it is unnecessary, even a waste of money, and that prices could be cut if there was no advertising. This will be discussed later, but at this early point it is useful to remind the reader that the historical and economic process
45 described before is now taking place in the **industrializing countries** of the "South". The extent of advertising marks the development and prosperity of a country.

Reading Comprehension

Exercise 1	Part 1

Read Part 1 silently, and then answer these questions.

1. Where do goods start?

    _____

2. Where do goods end?

    _____

3. Is advertising a part of marketing?

    _____

4. What does advertising reflect?

    _____

Exercise 2	Part 2

Read Part 2 silently, and then determine whether each statement is true or false according to the text.

1. Industrial countries do not need advertising.

    _____

2. Developing countries need advertising.

    _____

3. Signs are one way of advertising.

    _____

4. We need less advertising because population is increasing.

    _____

Listening Comprehension

Exercise 3 | Part 3

Close your book, and listen to your instructor reading   Part 3. Then answer these questions.

1. Were horse buses used for advertising?

    _____

2. Do producers need advertising?

    _____

3. Why do producers need advertising?

    _____

4. Does advertising lead to the increase of prices?

    _____

Vocabulary

Exercise 4 | Word Matching

Match words similar in meaning in the two lists.

List A		List B
1. manufacturer	_____	a. growing
2. consumer	_____	b. hotel
3. developing	_____	c. strong
4. inn	_____	d. maker
5. powerful	_____	e. user
		f. process
		g. shopkeeper

Exercise 5 | Noun Derivation

> Nouns are usually derived from verbs and adjectives by adding a suitable suffix, e.g., dictation, greatness. Such suffixes are called **noun-forming suffixes**, e.g., -ion, -ence, -ity, -ness, -er, -ment.

Derive a noun from each of these words.

1. distribute _____   6. useful _____

2. depend _____   7. produce _____

3. modern _____   8. continuous _____

4. survive _____   9. hold _____

5. live _____   10. reflect _____

Exercise 6 | Antonyms

> Antonyms can be derived by adding a suitable prefix, e.g., **un-, in-, mis-, dis-**.

Give the opposites of these words by prefixing or giving a different word.

1. development _____   6. profit _____

2. expansion _____   7. easy _____

3. known _____   8. necessary _____

4. effective _____   9. dependent _____

5. buyer _____   10. able _____

Grammar

Exercise 7 | Prepositions

Re-read the first paragraph of Part 1 carefully, and underline the prepositions there. List them here as well.

Exercise 8 | The Impossible Condition

> *The **impossible condition** deals with the past, e.g., If I **had seen** him, I **would have told** him. The condition did not happen, and, thus, the result did not happen either.*

Combine each pair of sentences using if.

1. He didn't study. He didn't pass the test.

---

2. He didn't work hard. He didn't get high grades.

---

3. They didn't invite him. He didn't come.

---

4. He didn't get up early. He didn't catch the bus.

Exercise 9 | Active ⟹ Passive

> *To change the present continuous verb from the active to the passive, we use this structure: **am/is/are+being+Form 3**, e.g., is writing ⟹ is being written.*

Change these sentences from the active to the passive.

1. He is distributing goods now.

_____

2. They are advertising their products.

_____

3. The factory is producing large quantities this year.

_____

4. He is discussing the matter with his parents.

_____

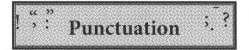

! " " : Punctuation ; ?

| Exercise 10 | Mark Addition |

Add punctuation marks and capital letters wherever necessary.

1. after the product is made it needs naming packing pricing and distribution

_____

2. developing countries work hard to come closer to developed countries

_____

3. where he is now is not known

_____

4. the pacific ocean is larger than the atlantic ocean

_____

5. the dead sea is the lowest area on the earth

_____

Spelling **and** Dictation

ABCDEFGHI JKLMN   OPQRSTUV WXYZ

Exercise 11   *All* Combined

*When **all** is combined with another word, one l is dropped, e.g., already.*

Combine these two units into one word.

1. all + ready   _____   5. all + ways   _____

2. all + right   _____   6. all + though   _____

3. all + together   _____   7. all + so   _____

4. all + mighty   _____   8. all + most   _____

Exercise 12   Practice

Practice the spelling of these words.

1. advertise   _____   6. services   _____

2. industrial   _____   7. media   _____

3. organization   _____   8. require   _____

4. product   _____   9. criticize   _____

5. developing   _____   10. complain   _____

Exercise 13   Dictation

You may have any paragraph in the passage or a part of it as a dictation exercise, depending on your instructor's choice.

_____

_____

Pronunciation

Exercise 14   c → s

> The letter **c** before **i** or **e** is pronounced /s/, e.g., *civil, century*. Otherwise, it is /k/, e.g., *claim, cottage*.

Pronounce these words, and show whether c is pronounced /s/ or /k/.

1. city _____   6. cinema _____

2. cottage _____   7. coat _____

3. cell _____   8. cut _____

4. current _____   9. certain _____

5. care _____   10. cat _____

Exercise 15   Stress

Pronounce and re-write these words, putting the strong stress on the right syllable, e.g., cólour.

1. maintain _____   6. require _____

2. describe _____   7. economic _____

3. prosperity _____   8. discuss _____

4. extent _____   9. survive _____

5. century _____   10. customer _____

✍ Free Writing ✍

| Exercise 16 | Paragraph Writing |

Write a ten-line paragraph about the need for advertising in marketing. The topic sentence may be like this: Advertising is essential for modern marketing.

_____

_____

_____

_____

_____

_____

_____

_____

_____

_____

Unit 14

Man and Science

(1)

The achievements of science in providing physical comforts and **means of relaxation** – shorter hours of labor, more abundant and better food, more adequate clothing and housing, fast and comfortable **means of communication**, a greater variety of amusements – are often disparaged with the remark that they do not necessarily make for greater happiness. True, they do not; but are these **achievements**, on the whole, not either conditions or adjuncts of happier and worthier living? Have they not **relieved** us of the negative effect of too much work, made child labor unnecessary and universal education possible?

Scientific research and the **applications** of science in the course of fifty years have increased four-fold the **productivity** of labor and have doubled the length of life. Science has made it possible for each to work at **routine tasks** half as long as formerly and at the same time to consume twice as much wealth as formerly. Fourteen hours of labor, shared by women and children, once provided hovels, lice, and black bread for most people, **luxury** for a few. Seven hours of labor will now supply comfortable homes, warm clothes, and healthful food for all. If the resources provided by science were properly

distributed, there would be **sufficient wealth** to enable all to share in the

desirable luxuries that science has created, and to enjoy in full measure the most
nearly ultimate goods of life: home, friends, things to do, freedom, and **self-respect**.

(2)

Our dependence on science for happiness is perhaps more obvious in the
prevention and cure of disease than in the production of physical comfort. We
need not speak of the dentist and the **oculist** although the magnitude of their
service to humanity is beyond estimation. The losses, suffering, and degradation
spared humanity by the application of recent surgical and **bacteriological
knowledge** is a more impressive item of our debt to science. Remove the
means of **disinfection** now at our service and 15% instead of 1% of the
patients would pass from the **operating table** to the grave. Not long ago, the

mortality from diphtheria was 80%; it is now reduced to a very small figure. Only parents who have watched a beloved child struggling with death will be able to conjecture what that single item may mean in relief from **mental torture**.

(3)

Is it necessary to draw up a list of other scourges mastered by **medical science**: smallpox, yellow fever, hydrophobia, tetanus, sleeping sickness, syphilis, leprosy? These and other diseases, responsible in the past for a very large part of the losses and suffering of humanity, are now under complete or **partial control**.

No less wonderful than the success of science in checking or eliminating **microbic diseases** are the discoveries in connection with the functions of the **endocrine glands**. These glands, the thyroid in the neck, the pituitary at the base of the skull, the adrenal above the kidneys, and many others, secrete substances (**hormones**) which modify the structure or function of certain organs. The baby born with an inadequate thyroid gland is a misshapen, drooling little being with protruding tongue and **abdomen**. He becomes a stunted, bandy legged imbecile. But if early enough he be given **thyroid extract**, he will probably develop into a normal human being.

Reading Comprehension

Exercise 1 | **Part 1**

Read Part 1 silently, and then determine whether each statement is true or false according to the text.

1. Some people believe that science achievements do not necessarily make our life happier.

    _____

2. Science has increased daily work hours.

    _____

3. Science has increased the productivity of our work.

    _____

4. Now, thanks to science, we work fourteen hours per day.

    _____

5. Science has advanced a lot in the last fifty years.

    _____

Exercise 2 | **Part 2**

Read Part 2 silently, and then answer these questions.

1. What was the percentage of deaths in surgical operations?

    _____

2. What is it now owing to scientific progress?

    _____

3. What was the death rate because of diphtheria?

    _____

4. Have dentists offered little service to humanity?

    _____

5. Has progress in surgery saved man from a lot of suffering?

Listening Comprehension

Exercise 3   Part 3

Close your book, and listen to your instructor reading   Part 3. Then answer these questions.

1. Could science overcome smallpox?

2. What is hydrophobia?

3. What kind of gland is the thyroid?

4. What do endocrine glands secrete?

5. Where is the adrenal gland?

6. Where is the pituitary gland?

Vocabulary

Exercise 4   Word Matching

Match the words of similar meanings in the two lists.

List A		List B
1. labor	_____	**a.** final
2. abundant	_____	**b.** duration
3. remark	_____	**c.** work
4. length	_____	**d.** previously
5. formerly	_____	**e.** comment
6. sufficient	_____	**f.** enough
7. ultimate	_____	**g.** plentiful
		h. eliminate

Exercise 5	**Adjective Derivation**

Derive an adjective from each word.

1. comfort	_____	6. effect	_____
2. variety	_____	7. knowledge	_____
3. condition	_____	8. humanity	_____
4. science	_____	9. substance	_____
5. produce	_____	10. prevention	_____

Exercise 6	**Word Production**

Give one word for each phrase. The first letter of the answer is given.

1. working against diseases before they happen: p _____.

2. a doctor specialized in teeth: d _____.

3. a specialist in the eyes: o _____.

4. a specialist in surgical operations: s _____.

5. a disease that chokes children: d _____.

6.   the secretion of endocrine glands: h _____.

Grammar

Exercise 7 | Reported Questions

> *Questions beginning with an auxiliary require adding **if** or **whether** when they are changed into reported speech, e.g., **Do** you know the answer? ⟹ He asked her **if** she knew the answer.*

Change these direct questions into indirect or reported ones.

1.   Have you done your homework?

     He asked me _____

2.   Can you do it?

     _____

3.   Will your friend come to the party tomorrow?

     _____

4.   Are you in good health now?

     _____

5.   Is he studying hard these days?

     _____

Exercise 8 | A Special Pattern

Change these sentences using this pattern: *The cost is $10 a bag.*

1.   Each car of these costs $10,000.

     _____

2.   Each book costs $30.

     _____

3.   Each apartment costs $30,000.

4.   Each kilogram costs $20.

5.   Each volume costs $15.

Exercise 9	The other one(s)

Add to each sentence a pattern like this: I want the other one(s), **using the same verb in the sentence.**

1.   I don't want to buy this car.

2.   He doesn't like to review these books.

3.   She doesn't prefer this dress.

4.   They don't want to eat these apples.

5.   I don't like to read such novels.

Exercise 10	Mark Addition

Add the suitable punctuation marks wherever necessary, without forgetting capital letters.

this opportunity was made to help in three further ways first he was able to put in a great deal of time reading at the detroit public library between trains secondly finding that he could sell other peoples newspapers he thought he would start one of his own and did printing it on the train and making it up from bits of local information he picked up on the line thirdly without asking anyones permission, he set up a laboratory in the van where his papers were carried

_____

_____

_____

_____

_____

_____

_____

_____

ABCDEFGHI JKLMN	**Spelling and Dictation**	OPQRSTUV WXYZ

Exercise 11	ie or ei

> We usually have **ie**, not **ei**, except after **c**, e.g., *receive*, or when the vowel is pronounced like **late**, e.g., *eight*.

Are the missing letters in these words ie or ei?

1. rec __ ve   _____   6. w __ gh   _____

2. dec __ ve   _____   7. bel __ f   _____

3. th __ f   _____   8. n __ ghbor   _____

4. rel __ f   _____   9. c __ ling   _____

5. w __ ght   _____   10. br __ f   _____

Exercise 12	Practice

Practice the spelling of these words.

1. abundant   _____   6. hormone   _____

2. luxury   _____   7. endocrine   _____

3. measure   _____   8. eliminate   _____

4. smallpox   _____   9. infection   _____

5. adequate   _____   10. estimation   _____

Exercise 13	Dictation

You may have any paragraph in the passage or a part of it as a dictation exercise, depending on your instructor's choice.

_____

_____

_____

_____

Pronunciation

Exercise 14	The Final *mb*

*When **mb** is final, **b** is silent, e.g., bomb.*

Pronounce these words, and re-write them, putting a dot under any silent letter.

1. *bomb*   _____   5. *climb*   _____

2. *comb*   _____   6. *thumb*   _____

3. *tomb*   _____   7. *womb*   _____

4. *dumb*   _____   8. *rub*   _____

Exercise 15	Stress

Pronounce and re-write these words, putting the strong stress on the right syllable, e.g., yéllow.

1. beyond   _____   6. torture   _____

2. medical   _____   7. remove   _____

3. function   _____   8. suffering   _____

4. modify   _____   9. humanity   _____

5. mortality   _____   10. responsible   _____

✍ Free Writing ✍

Exercise 16	Paragraph Writing

Write a ten-line paragraph about the achievements of science. The topic sentence may look like this: The achievements of science have made a great difference in our life.

_____

_____

_____

_____

_____

_____

_____

_____

_____

_____

Text Sources

Unit 1.   Thornley, G.C. *Scientific English Practice*. London: Longmans, Green and Co Ltd. (pp. 19-21).

Unit 2.   Finch, R.J. *Practical Geography*. London: Evans Brothers Ltd, 1995. (pp. 15-17).

Unit 3.   Thornley, G.C. *Scientific English Practice*. London: Longmans, Green and Co Ltd. (pp. 42-43).

Unit 4.   Alkhuli, M.A. *An Introduction to Linguistics*. Amman: Dar Alfalah, 1997. (pp. 142-144).

Unit 5.   Ward, E.H. *Senior Physics* (Part 1). London: Thomas Nelson & Sons Ltd, 1995. (pp. 3-5).

Unit 6.   Alkhuli, M.A. *English Phonetics and Phonology*. Amman: Dar Alfalah, 2002. (pp. 25-28).

Unit 7.   Lowery, R.C. *Supervisory Management*. New Jersey: Prentice-Hall, 1995. (pp. 5-7).

Unit 8.   Brownline, I. *Basic Documents on Human Rights*. London: Clarendon Press, 1993. (pp. 22-23).

Unit 9.   Stamp, L.D. *Discovery Geography*. London: Longman, 1990. (pp. 30-31).

Unit 10.   Macra, S. *Public Administration: An Introduction*. New York: English Language Book Society, 1990. (pp. 8-9).

Unit 11.   Verne, J. *Around the World in Eighty Days*. London: Penguin Books, 1994. (pp. 9-10).

Unit 12.   Akmajian, A. *Linguistics*. London: The MIT Press, 1995. (pp. 5-6).

Unit 13.   Jefkins, F. *Advertising*. Plymouth: Macdonald and Evans, 1995. (pp. 1-2).

Unit 14.   Leuba, J.H. *God or Man*. London: Kegan Paul, Tench, Trubner and Co, Ltd, 1994. (pp. 87-89).

The Author's English Books

1. *A Dictionary of Islamic Terms: English-Arabic & Arabic-English*

2. *Simplified English Grammar*

3. *A Dictionary of Education: English- Arabic*

4. *A Dictionary of Theoretical Linguistics: English-Arabic*

5. *A Dictionary of Applied Linguistics: English-Arabic*

6. *Teaching English to Arab Students*

7. *A Workbook for English Teaching Practice*

8. *Programmed TEFL Methodology*

9. *The Teacher of English*

10. *Improve Your English*

11. *A Workbook for English*

12. *○Advance Your English*

13. *An Introduction to Linguistics*

14. *Comparative Linguistics: English and Arabic*

15. *A Contrastive Transformational Grammar: English-Arabic*

16. *The Light of Islam*

17. *The Need for Islam*

18. *Traditions of Prophet Muhammad /B1*

19. *Traditions of Prophet Muhammad /B2*

20. *The Truth about Jesus Christ*

21. *Islam and Christianity*

22. *Questions and Answers about Islam*

23. *Learn Arabic by Yourself*

24. *The Blessing of Islam*

25.   *Why have they chosen Islam?*

26.   *The Crisis of Western Civilization*

27.   *A Comparison between the Four Gospels*

28.   *Methods of Teaching English at the Elementary Stage*

29.   *Methods of Teaching English*

30.   *Teaching English as a Foreign Language*

31.   *Islamic Faith*

32.   *Human Rights in Islam*

33.   *Penal Codes in Islam*

34.   *The Pillars of Islam*

35.   *Morality in Islam*

36.   *The Woman in Islam*

37.   *The Only Right Choice: Islam*

38.   *What do you know about Islam?*

39.   *The Straight Path: Islam*

40.   *Legal Translation: From English into Arabic*

41.   *Humanities Translation: From English into Arabic*

42.   *Science Translation: From English into Arabic*

43.   *General Translation: From English into Arabic*

44.   *Literary Translation: From English into Arabic*

45.   *Mass-Media Translation: From English into Arabic*

46.   *Administration and Finance Translation: From English into Arabic*

47.   *An Introduction to Semantics*

48.   *English Phonetics and Phonology*

49.   *English Skills Two*

50.   *English Grammar: Morphology*

Printed in the United States
By Bookmasters